Lost Parents

When Our Children Leave This World Too Soon

MICHAEL WILKERSON

WESTBOW
PRESS®
A DIVISION OF THOMAS NELSON
& ZONDERVAN

WestBow Press books may be ordered through booksellers or by contacting:

WestBow Press
A Division of Thomas Nelson & Zondervan
1663 Liberty Drive
Bloomington, IN 47403
www.westbowpress.com
1 (866) 928-1240

ISBN: 978-1-9736-2575-9 (sc)
ISBN: 978-1-9736-2574-2 (e)

Library of Congress Control Number: 2018904453

Print information available on the last page.

WestBow Press rev. date: 5/11/2018

This book is dedicated to my daughter, Kendra.

It is your love and God's hand on my shoulder that gave me the courage to write this story. I know you would tell me not to make a big deal over you. I hope you understand that this is your legacy, your belief in giving to others and helping those who are in need. My hope is that someone who has to take the same journey will find something to help them make it one more step. I dedicate this book to you, Sister.

Love, Dad

Contents

Preface

Our daughter Kendra was thirty-two years old and about seven months pregnant when a viral infection entered her body. The illness attacked her respiratory system taking her into a critical race to stop the infection and restore her health. The virus spread through her body quickly. Her fever was sudden and severe. The illness progressed at such a dangerous rate that the baby would be compromised if a delivery procedure was not initiated immediately.

At 12:12 a.m. on November 12, 2013, Meredith Fendt was born at Sacred Heart Hospital in Pensacola, Florida. An hour later, a jet from the University of Alabama Birmingham (UAB) landed at Pensacola International Airport to take Kendra to Birmingham where she could get medical care not available in Pensacola. UAB's medical specialist team provided care to stem the ravages the severe virus was taking on her body. Meredith remained in the Neonatal Intensive Care United (NICU) at Sacred Heart.

I never thought about writing anything concerning our experience with Kendra. Writing happened quite by accident. A young lady at our church developed a Facebook page titled "Praying for Kendra Fendt." During our first week in Birmingham with Kendra I began to write a journal. Most days I wrote twice a day because we had meetings or received new information concerning Kendra's status and the medical plan for her in the morning and afternoon. This book is part of my own therapy to let go of so much that I have held onto for the past four years. I will tell you, I would never have chosen to write this painful memory.

As Kendra's dad, my experience as a hospital homebound teacher in Pensacola exposed me to another side of life. Most children never have to be hospitalized. Those children who are hospitalized enter a world unlike what most children will ever have to experience. Their parents are plunged into a mental and emotional abyss, nothing like the life they once knew. Many of the children I worked with were chronically ill or medically complex with congenital diseases or other serious problems. I saw how the lives of these children and their families were so deeply affected by their difficulties in and out of the hospital. A few children did not survive. I saw how the loss of a child was so devastating that some marriages did not survive. Life was forever altered and nothing these families knew was ever the same.

As a teacher and a dad, I was grateful every day for my daughter Kendra and my wife Shirley. When Kendra fell in love and married Ed Fendt, he was woven into an integral part of our family. Ed's dad Hank and his stepmother Penny were welcomed into our family as so much more to us than in-laws.

While we were in Birmingham, various people entered our lives and provided comfort, prayer and practical needs. We were too worried or involved in our thoughts and prayers for Kendra's well-being to stop and take care of ourselves.

Writing this book began a journey into a place that I have struggled to escape. In order to complete the task, I had to revisit moments to which I did not want to return. The risk was triggering the PTSD (post-traumatic stress disorder) I developed after we lost Kendra. The risk opened wounds that were barely healed and other wounds that were still aching. And yet the greatest risk was not writing this story. I truly believe this journey has to be open where others can see where it began, where it has gone and where it is now.

There are two reasons I have reached this point in my life. First was my faith in God. Despite how our journey has unfolded, everything I believe about leaning on God is still where I find my strength. The second reason in writing this book is it may help someone else who has to experience the death of a loved one. I grieve in hope that someone will find something in this writing that will help them. If that happens, it is the spirit of our Lord speaking to them. There can be no other reason for writing such a personally destructive part of my life for anyone to see.

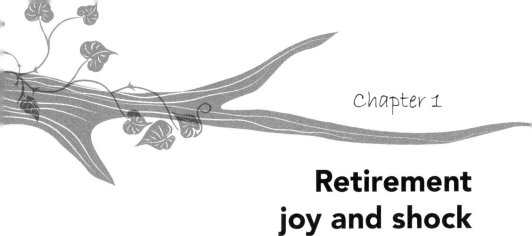

Chapter 1

Retirement joy and shock

Life is a journey. While every one of us experiences our own unique journey, other people help us navigate through life. It takes time to become aware of the situations and moments that we have in common with others. In the midst of turning a page in my life to begin a new chapter, life took an unbelievable turn no one wants to face.

Our daughter Kendra was in the beginning of her seventh month of pregnancy with her first child. Both Kendra and her husband Ed worked full-time jobs. Ed was taking care of Kendra as the joy of their lives neared the time for delivery. As I boarded a cruise ship to live out one of my long held dreams, life took its own lead. Everything we anticipated was unexpected and caused fear that we could never have imagined.

In the coming days and weeks, my wife Shirley, her sister Wanda, and her husband Bobby were all part of our journey offering love and standing in for us as we traveled this dark road with Kendra. Hank and Penny Fendt, Ed's dad and stepmother, were the anchors who held all of us together through what they did for Ed and Kendra. Stephanie, Wanda's daughter, moved into our home and took care of our dog, Myrtle. Clain Roberts, our music pastor at Immanuel Baptist Church in Pace along with his wife Cindy, supported us and drove the distance a number of times to see us with Kendra in the hospital. Where we were going many had gone before us. Where we would end up, only we would understand as this was our journey alone except for the presence of God and the spirit.

November 1st, 2013

Kendra came by to see us before we left for San Juan, Puerto Rico. She didn't stay long, or long enough for me. She wished us a wonderful cruise and updated us on her pregnancy. In utero, baby Meredith was developing just fine and except for occasional backaches and other common side effects of pregnancy, Kendra was doing okay. She said her sinuses bothered her and she felt a little tired. Shirley and I told her to take care of herself and call the doctor if she felt any worse. I hugged Sister, told her how much I loved her, and we would see her when we returned from the cruise.

November 3rd, 2013

"For months, my mom and aunt have been planning this moment for dad's retirement cruise! He was just surprised by his younger brother on the ship!! They will all sail away tonight from San Juan on a 7 day tour of the Southern Caribbean."

This was the last entry Kendra wrote on her Facebook page.

Shirley and my brother's wife Linda planned this get-together for a cruise to the southern Caribbean for months. This vacation celebrated my thirty-seven years of teaching. My career began in 1976 and on October 30th, 2013, I retired from my last position as a hospital homebound teacher in the Escambia County School district in Northwest Florida. I taught school in a number of capacities over the years and because of the kindness of another special education teacher, Jan DeStafney, I learned of an opening for a teacher in the homebound program. I held dual certification in Elementary Education and K through 12 Exceptional Education in the state of Florida. I interviewed for the homebound position in December 1999. On January 15th, I began teaching in my last position as a public school teacher. From January 2000 to October 2013, I taught homebound and hospitalized children in a job I loved. The time flew by and now I was looking back at how life rolled along so quickly.

Kendra's Facebook entry indicated I was surprised by my brother and his wife on board our cruise ship. I was so surprised I couldn't react because I called my brother a few weeks before just to talk about going with us on the cruise. He told me it wasn't possible. Now here he stood with his wife Linda, and my happiness could not be expressed in words or emotions. I simply stood there, frozen.

Our cruise took us away from the world we lived in, away from the everyday routine. For me, the cruise punctuated the end of my teaching career and the beginning of a new chapter in my life. My wife Shirley was with me, my brother and his wife were with me, and I was going to see places I always wanted to see. At home, our only child Kendra was happily married to her husband Ed and living the dream of first-time parents, expecting a little girl on the way some time in December. Rarely had I felt so good about life. I dared to look ahead to December, maybe Christmas Day, when our granddaughter Meredith would enter this world.

We sailed out of San Juan at night, past the Castillo San Felipe Morro and its tall stone walls. Night enveloped us and the lights over the Castillo faded away as we sailed into our adventure. It was a long time since I felt the satisfaction of enjoying life as I was at that moment. Here I was standing on the foredeck of a ship peering into the darkness and viewing the stars that were bright and clear above me. I did not have to get up at 5:30 a.m., drive into work and review my plans for the students I would visit in their homes. Lunch would not be out of a sack at my desk or on the run going from one home to the next. Tonight I was eating in a wonderful dining room with my family.

My only plans were to avoid making plans. Other than the tours and adventures at some of our island stops, I had no plans except to enjoy myself, enjoy being with Shirley and have a lot of laughs with my brother and sister-in-law. Shirley and Linda planned the trip so well. Our rooms were two doors from each other on the same level. We toured Barbados and St. Thomas. As couples, we visited the cities and shops on our own and talked about our experiences each evening at dinner.

Our first stop was St. Thomas, an American territory, one of four islands that form the U.S. Virgin islands. We departed the ship and joined a tour group. Our day was good, seeing the island from an open-sided bus. The view above Magens Bay was beautiful. The deep blues and emerald greens of the ocean highlighted the white beaches and the deep green hillsides on the island. In town, we ate at a nice restaurant and had some seafood which I always enjoy. Before we knew it, we were back on the ship setting sail for Barbados. That evening, we talked about our adventure and the sights we saw. Dinner was wonderful, a nice ending to an event-filled day. I went to bed feeling so good about our trip and the sights that were waiting for us on the islands we had yet to visit.

On St. Kitts, Shirley and I took a tour in the rainforest. We saw trees of tremendous girth and height. The atmosphere was not as humid and uncomfortable as we expected. Our guide told us monkeys lived in the trees and there were no poisonous snakes on the ground. The forest offered food for those who knew what to look for along with cocoa pods on the trees growing wild in the forest. We climbed a steep hill holding onto a rope that brought us to the top of a ridge. As we walked along, we saw more tropical plants including a tree that was encrusted with thorns from its base to the top of its trunk. Our walk built up a hunger and thirst in all of us. We were the oldest people on the tour and the younger people were kind, waiting for us to catch up to them. We walked along the crest back to the starting point where our guide gave us a delicious lunch of fresh fruits, pulled pork, juices, rum punch and the most delicate sugar cookies I have ever tasted. Our trip back to the ship followed the shoreline and we looked out on the vast expanse of the Caribbean Sea. We imagined Spanish and English explorers hundreds of years ago seeing the island for the first time.

The views of islands and sunsets as we traveled south in the Caribbean allowed me to relax for the first time in many years. My mind was no longer on work, money, or making a living. I was thinking about some of the things I planned to do for years such as kayaking part of the Suwannee and visiting the springs in the winter when the manatees congregate over the warm water pouring out of the limestone fissures. Time would be savored, no longer measured by an hour in one child's home and the rush to get from one side of town to the other quickly and safely to see my next student. No, I was not missing work at that moment, nor the endless amount of paperwork and the self-evaluations that the state mandated for all teachers.

I would miss the children and how they took on life despite the pain of their ailments. I was humbled by their response to living with cancer or cystic fibrosis or other terrible attacks on their bodies and minds. I would miss my peers in Hospital Homebound especially Wanda Rankin, Kathy Steinbeck, Cindy Taylor, and Carolyn Jones who retired a couple of years before me. They were strong and wonderful teachers, each with their own unique skills and the strength to deal with tragedy in their own lives. I cared about them but rarely showed it like I could have. I would make sure to see them after retirement. They forgave my temperamental battles with paperwork which sometimes resulted in bruised feelings. These are friends who are rare, to forgive and still help me.

My Exceptional Student Education supervisor, Teri Szafran, guided me with patience that few would have with a person like me. I was impatient with some of the rules that were so rigid for our children and scoffed at what I saw as a blanket approach regarding testing and other requirements. Teri was fair with me, guiding me through the firmness and knowledge that she possessed concerning my responsibilities and position. My homebound supervisor Susan Cole and I had a lot in common. We both had daughters named Kendra. Though we graduated from different colleges, we entered teaching at nearly the same time. Susan also possessed understanding and patience with me and more than a few times listened to my prattle about some of the requirements that seemed so out of touch with the difficulties homebound children face every day.

I was blessed to be surrounded by good people, mostly Christian people who loved their work and the kids they worked with each day. One could work with a mentally challenged child one hour, then the next hour work with a fully capable child with cerebral palsy who could not speak but could get one's attention quickly in other ways. My work was never the same. It never seemed completed. Some children I would see for years, others no more than a month or two. Children came and went, some healing, some who would never heal, and some who would leave this world too soon. I did not take time to think about what life would be like after I retired. I wanted to continue to work with my children just as if I would never leave. They deserved that from me. I tried not to start any new programs so that their new teachers would be able to make their own evaluations and teach the children in the way that complimented their talents. Homebound children who have been with me for a while need time to adjust to other teachers, or at least that was what I thought. I planned to check with their teachers in a few months and see how everyone was adjusting. Younger teachers bring different ideas and hopefully better methods for some things that I was doing. I was never afraid of doing things different if they would help a child learn better.

So here I was somewhere near the 14th parallel north and I was thinking about my students. It was time to let go of their individual education plans and think about what I could do that would be useful and something I wanted to do. I looked at the seas and focused on the air touching my skin with the warmth of a November evening far from the coolness of home back in Pace, Florida. Our ship would dock in the morning and we would set out on another adventure, this time sailing into the aquamarine tinted waters of St. Martin.

We debarked in St. Martin, our last stop before our ship returned to San Juan, Puerto Rico the next day. We walked out from the pier area and caught a taxi to take us across the island to our sailboat. We spent the day on the water sailing and relaxing in the inland waters. Our host was a woman who sailed all over the Caribbean and knew what she was doing. We saw amazing shorelines of limestone. At one point, we watched an airliner skim over the end of a runway that was populated with scores of people experiencing the thrill and tense moments of the closeness of the aircraft.

During our sail, I walked out on the bowsprit and experienced the beauty of watching the bow cut through the waves below me. Water sprayed up sometimes on my feet and legs cooling me in the mid-day sun. The bow rode into the waves and then over the waves much like the feel of a car going over a small rise and quickly dropping on the descent. It took me awhile to gain a sense of balance. Once I figured out the rhythm of the water and the boat's rising and falling, I felt a sensory lulling of the mind and body. I enjoyed hanging out ahead of the boat looking down through the guard rail and the wooden planks. I relished the feeling of being both a part of the boat and apart from the world. The horizon rose and fell, aligning me with its level and then pushing me above or below the level.

The wind and water, sun and fresh air uplifted me not only in my physical sense but in my mind and heart. I was not looking forward to retirement. I did not embrace the idea of being out of work though I welcomed the change. Here a week into my cruise vacation, I began to accept the idea that I could shape my retirement into a purposeful life beyond the daily hours of clocks and paperwork. There was much to do and with careful planning and prudent handling of our assets, Shirley and I could enjoy this next chapter in our lives.

On fair days like we had in St. Martin, I could imagine how a sailor might be able to clear his mind on a sailing craft. No salt water sheets of spray stinging the skin and crusting the decks. No wind whistling in the ropes and roaring in the sails. No ship bones creaking and moaning as the hull pounded into the tons of pressure as frothing waves rammed into each beam and board. It took a certain kind of person to sail in the bowels of a raging ocean. If he didn't respect the sea, he would learn to respect the sea or face his fate.

On our return to the dock after a wonderful day of sailing and eating on the deck, we watched a small rainstorm move inland. We sailed the edge of the rainstorm and as we watched, a three-mast sailing ship move into the rain. Its black and white sides reminded me of the days of frigates and brigantines. Our day was complete, sailing along seeing jets and huge mansions while visions of a time gone by slipped through the veil of rain to anchor in a cove that might have seen a thousand other sailing ships in its time.

That evening, we all talked about our week of adventures and the things we had seen while sailing across the southern islands of the Caribbean. Our time together with my brother and his wife are precious and rare. My brothers live far away and vacation time together is something we have tried to work out many times. Our work schedules, the distance between our homes and other complications made gathering for vacation difficult. This was a wonderful present to me from Shirley to have my brother and Linda join us. I was overwhelmed when they surprised me on the ship. Now I realized just how special having us all together impacted me. I loved spending time with them. In the morning, we docked in San Juan and spent an extra day exploring the old city. That same day I was thinking soon I would have a beautiful granddaughter and my daughter would fulfill her dream of being a mother.

November 10th, 2013

Shirley and I made our way to our hotel in the old city of San Juan. It was a unique place with a Middle Eastern theme. The movie Casablanca gave the hotel its name. We made our way up the stairs and checked into our room. Then out the door we went to explore the old city. There is an amazing amount of architectural history in San Juan. Old buildings beam bright in pastel and primary colors. Spanish arches, ironwork and tiled roofs gave us a feeling we were in Europe, not on an island flanked by the Atlantic on the north shore and the Caribbean Sea on the south shore.

We visited El Morro, the great fort that guards the entry into the Bay of San Juan. Its walls rose high above our heads, formidable looking even in this day and age. The fort was constructed in the late 1400's and was enlarged as Spanish power built in the new world. It is an amazing place to visit along with the old city walls and another fort, San Cristobal. Our day was full of views of the beautiful old city as we walked along the fortress walls and strolled on some of the still existing blue cobblestone streets. Tired from our afternoon walk, we returned to our room, freshened up and went out to eat.

We called home for the first time during our cruise to see how Kendra was doing. Shirley was quiet when she got off the phone and the smile I had seen for so many days was gone. Kendra was home with a fever and had been to the doctor twice with her physical health still compromised. All of the days we spent on the cruise and in San Juan collided with the reality of Kendra's needs. We were over 1500 miles from home and our daughter and her husband were facing serious issues that we had no way to help them. Even more demoralizing was that we were not leaving until late afternoon the next day. In my entire life, I had only felt as helpless and out of place one other time. That was when my mother was rushed to the emergency room when her body began to fail. I was out of phone range on the west side of Pensacola, a mile or two from the Alabama border when someone from my office finally got in touch with me to let me know my mother was in crisis. It was a seventy mile drive from Pensacola to where my mother was in Niceville, Florida. I did not make it in time to see her and now I had great fear that my daughter was not doing well and again I was not near to be with her.

26 In the same way the spirit helps us in our weakness. We do not know what we ought to pray for, but the spirit himself intercedes for us with groans that words cannot express. 27 And he who searches our hearts knows the mind of the Spirit, because the spirit intercedes for the saints in accordance with God's will. Romans 8: 26- 27 NIV

In effect, Paul was telling the Romans to ask the Holy Spirit to help each of them by praying to God to help us with the right words. These are words that address God's will, the only real thoughts and wants that would truly be answered. I prayed in the best way I knew for Kendra because I sensed that her needs were fearful. I knew that I needed to be in control of my feelings. I prayed for calmness, wisdom, and patience to make good decisions without emotions leading me or my heart clouding. I needed guidance to know what to do if our situation was as precarious as my feelings led me to believe. I had a day and evening to think about what to do. What I could do was wait for time to pass and new information that would help all of us bear the weight of our concerns and distress over the unknown.

Paul's directions gave me time to compose myself. While I did not think specifically of Romans, I turned to what I remembered and kept it in my mind.

Trust in the Lord with all your heart and lean not on your own understanding. Proverbs 3: 5

I did not understand why Kendra and her baby were in such danger. I could not know how this trauma affected her husband Ed. I would be extremely worried and fearful if Shirley were ill and having problems breathing. I knew little about Kendra's sickness and it had my full attention. My years teaching in the local children's hospital in Pensacola taught me a lot about what can happen to a person with various illnesses. While my knowledge was not as extensive as a medical person, I knew a lot more than most lay people about how illnesses progress. I had a rudimentary understanding of certain medications and methods of treating patients. I knew enough to feel I knew too much and entirely too little about what could be going on a gulf away from where I was.

My heart wanted to fight. I wanted to get home any way I could at that moment, but it simply wasn't possible. I wanted to take on the situation and aggressively stand in with Kendra and Ed as soon as I could. My prayers and the Holy Spirit took hold of me. I still wanted to fight. My mind told me to wait, to accept where I was and where Sister was which went against my feelings and character. Tired and worn out, I went to dinner with Shirley in the old town. We walked back to our room, few words spoken between us. Exhausted from thinking and the tense feelings that sometimes defined my demeanor when I had no control, I fell asleep at last in the darkness of night in the hands of our Lord.

November 11th, 2013

We woke and had breakfast in our hotel dining area. To pass the time we walked around town and had lunch. Since our flight was leaving about eight p.m., we had a lot of time to pass. The wait was excruciating. When one knows that there is another loved one in need of our love and confidence and we cannot give them what they need, it is an awful kind of suffering. Not only does one feel helpless, one might feel they are not doing what they should be doing. Emotions will take over where the mind should prevail. My mind was mentally in Puerto Rico while my heart was in Pensacola.

Our day passed in the beautiful sunshine and heat in Old San Juan. We called for a taxi and began our drive to the airport where we waited another four hours before our flight took off for Miami. The airport pulsed with the coming and going of aircraft. When a plane landed, the halls filled with busy travelers making their way into town or other places in Puerto Rico. Soon the halls were quiet again. A few people were scattered here and there. We walked in the terminal, looked in the shops, found a little something to eat, and waited. Breath after breath urged the sun to settle into the distance and we began to anticipate our flight to Miami.

Our flight from Puerto Rico to Miami took about two hours and forty minutes with an average speed of five hundred miles an hour. We traveled on a northwest flight path passing over the Turks and Caicos Islands and The Bahamas before we touched down in Miami. We were two-thirds of our way home to Pace. I have flown a bit in my day. My first flight was with my dad in his silver and red Piper plane when I was around four or five years old. I remember looking down at the Oklahoma landscape and the feeling of the warm air lifting and pulling on that little plane. I was scared, but only enough to know there was danger if something happened. My first flight was a success. My dad, a pilot and co-pilot, flew KC-135 tankers in the United States Air Force. As he did with his tankers, he delivered me and my older brother Steve safely back to the ground in Atlus, Oklahoma. It must have been around 1960. I would not fly again until 1964 when I would settle into a seat on a Pan Am flight from New Jersey to Mildenhall, England. In both cases, I was going somewhere I had never been.

Our flight to Miami was smooth. As we approached Miami, the light from the east coast of southern Florida illuminated the city areas north as far as one could see. I wondered if any of the people below me were afraid, scared like I was that the truth of what I had to learn was too much for me to understand. One is alone in this world, very alone sometimes when a city surrounds them. A feeling of isolation prevails when clouds of moisture hide the aircraft wings that carry every person on that plane home. There wasn't much that Shirley and I could say to each other. I prayed. She prayed. Together we hoped. We just wanted everything to be better.

Miami's airport was everything that San Juan wasn't: busy, loud, impersonal, big, and a place I wanted to leave as soon as I could. We walked across the airport to our gate where we boarded our next flight home. I left Shirley as she descended the stairs to the gate waiting area so I could take a break. When I got back to her, a familiar face was sitting with Shirley. David Keigley, a longtime friend, was on his way home from a business trip. His presence helped both of us because he was a person we knew and we could talk with him.

We had another hour to wait for our flight to Pensacola. We talked with David who was aware of Kendra's illness through his mother, Kay Keigley. Kay is a longtime friend from Kendra's days in the Pensacola Children's Chorus. The tension we felt for the last twenty-four hours let up a little because we were with a friend of our family and we wanted so much for everything to work out. The darkness that surrounded our little area only seemed to make the time slow down. We wondered when we would ever get on the small commuter jet that would take us home to Kendra and Ed.

Our impatience was suspended when there was finally a call to begin boarding the aircraft. It took about twenty minutes or so to board and then more time for the baggage. When the aircraft backed out and the engines were turning, it seemed like it took forever for the plane to taxi out from the gate and line up for its turn to take off. Finally, I could feel the engines turning and increasing up to the optimal power setting to begin the run down the flight line. The plane began slowly gaining speed. Then it seemed to jackrabbit into its run and we were off the ground flying over the opaque light laying below us and illuminating the horizon before us.

Kendra and Ed were married on a humid day when thunderstorms were scattered all about the Pensacola area. It was one of the happiest days of my life when they were married in St. Marks Methodist Church on Twelfth Avenue in Pensacola. I had rarely seen Kendra so happy and sure of what she was going to do. When the services began and I was standing outside of the sanctuary in the hall with Kendra. My eyes were misty. Knowing me so well, Kendra said, "Get it together Dad." It was the kick in the tail I needed. When we heard our cue through the music to come forward, we made the entry down the aisle toward the pulpit area.

I thought that was the longest walk I would ever make, but it was quick and in a way, too fast. I was giving my daughter away to her husband, Ed Fendt. I was old-fashioned. I believed that Ed was literally taking my daughter from me into his life. I trusted him to do right by Kendra and I expected Kendra to do right by Ed. Our friend and music director from our church in Pace, Clain Roberts, officiated the wedding ceremony. We were bursting with happiness for his presence and love for our daughter. My mind rambled on turning at a speed at least equal to the turbines on the jet winging us home. I thought about Kendra and the baby. I could not know the fear and confusion Ed was dealing with over the last twelve hours.

As we approached Pensacola, our plane began to drop into its approach from the north. I could see the lights of our small city. Where the lights faded, I could see Escambia Bay, dark and without depth, just a flat area in the view from my window. Behind us was Santa Rosa Island, guarding our city from the natural ravages of wind and tide and surf from the Gulf of Mexico. Our plane's wing flaps dropped. The engines began to whistle as the pilot jockeyed the power so that our landing was as smooth as possible. The aircraft drifted from the south, touching down with hardly a bump. Engines roared in reverse and the aircraft braked enough for each passenger to feel the weight of the aircraft strain against the dissipating inertia that carried us from Miami to Pensacola. As the jet slowed, the human activity within the plane picked up. People pulled out phones to call home or a friend. We soon arrived at our gate and Shirley pulled out her phone to contact Ed. The information we expected to hear was not what we had hoped.

Kendra was in Sacred Heart Hospital and the decision was made to perform a Cesarean delivery. In utero, baby Meredith was beginning to show signs of stress and Kendra was not getting better. Shirley's sister Wanda met us in the airport lobby and took her to Sacred Heart to be with Kendra. I took the pickup home that was parked at the airport and waited for Shirley to come home. We spoke with Ed and determined that we would drive the next morning to Birmingham, Alabama. Kendra's condition was such that the doctors determined that she would have a better chance of recovery if she was in the Cardiovascular Intensive Care Unit at the University of Alabama Birmingham Hospital. We were all tired and as we learned later, Ed was exhausted from loss of sleep over Kendra and the safety of their soon to be born daughter, Meredith.

So much happened in the days and hours after we knew Kendra was seriously ill. Our thinking had to be kept in a realm of facts. We had to try and reason with what we knew. Going beyond what was known would only cause more worry, more anxiety and lead to emotional decisions that would not help anyone. Shirley and I were tired. Flying from Puerto Rico to Miami and then to Pensacola only reinforced the feelings of helplessness we had. We were not home when Kendra's illness began and we were not there when she was taken into surgery. The helplessness we felt could overtake our ability to act and we didn't want to lose control over the one thing we could do. We could rest, pray and ready ourselves to go to Birmingham the next day. That we could do.

Chapter 2

The road to Birmingham

<u>November 13th, 2013</u>

Ed was so worn out that I took the wheel for our drive to Birmingham, Alabama from our home in Pace, Florida. The GPS in Ed's SUV indicated that we were 235 miles from our destination at the hospital. It estimated that we would be there in three hours and thirty minutes. I normally am not a fast driver. If the speed limit is 70 mph, I usually run 70 to 75 mph. That morning I drove 80 to 90 mph, whatever the road allowed me. I noted that only three cars passed me until we arrived in the rush hour traffic in Birmingham. I did not note when we arrived at the parking garage in Birmingham, but I know it was much sooner than what the GPS estimated we would average in our drive.

The University Of Alabama Medical Center is a conglomerate of buildings. Many of the buildings are joined by corridors that pass over avenues and streets connecting one building on one block with another building on another block. We walked out of the 4th Avenue parking deck into the North Pavilion. The hallway was wide enough for a four lane road. To a newcomer in the area, the buildings seemed cavernous at first view. We walked until we came to an information desk and asked for directions to the Cardiovascular ICU. That was where Kendra was. As tired as we were, we wanted to get to her as quickly as we could.

We began a series of walks along corridors, riding one elevator down to a lower floor and walking again. Then we caught another elevator up to another floor where Kendra was placed for her treatment. As we entered the CICU, only two of us could be in her room at a time. I waited while Ed and Shirley went in the room to see Kendra. As long as the flights from Puerto Rico and Miami had felt, the fifteen minutes or so that I waited to see Kendra bogged down into long resounding swings of a second hand on a large clock. The mind can become extremely imaginative during the waiting time.

I had seen many situations with children in critical condition during my working years in the Children's Unit at a pediatric hospital area in Pensacola. It is difficult to adjust to the sounds, the smells, and the medical equipment. For most people, it can be overwhelming and hard to comprehend at first sight. For me, each feeder line, each pump had a meaning and the medication feeding through those lines would tell me a lot about what the doctors were doing to treat Kendra's illness.

Visitors are allowed in the unit only so long. Hours were mostly reserved for the patients to rest and for the cardio teams to monitor and provide service for their patients. So many of the patients were recovering from major surgery or trauma events. It made sense to keep the visits to a minimum. Kendra's respiratory crisis brought her to this ICU unit. She was in isolation because of the still suspected but unconfirmed presence of influenza. We all had to take hazard precautions and dress appropriately in masks and hazard dressings. I had done this many times in my days teaching at the hospital in Pensacola. It only emphasized the seriousness of what I was about to see.

Shirley left Kendra's room and told me she was not awake but she was stable and her situation was changing from hour to hour. I walked into the CICU area where there were two rows of beds to my left in a room that looked to be about seventy-five feet long. Kendra was in an isolation room in the CICU. I put on the gown and a mask and went into the room. Kendra was asleep and her monitors were relatively quiet, a good sign in my mind. Her oxygen count was low and they were assisting her breathing. Various tubes and lines ran from an IV pole to her arms. Her hair was a bit unkempt, but I could tell Shirley tried to fix her appearance for her. Ed was sitting quietly in a chair opposite the side of the bed I was on.

I leaned into Sister and whispered in her ear how much I loved her. I told her to be strong and to keep believing, keep reaching out because she held the keys to her own recovery. I whispered a few other things and then

I began to cry. It was the first time I had cried any real amount in longer than I could remember. It was around 11:00 a.m. November 13th, 2013. Kendra was only hours ago on an operating table where her daughter was born about seven weeks early. About an hour later, a jet from UAB landed at Pensacola International Airport and shortly after one a.m. that jet took off with Kendra headed for Birmingham to deliver her to the CICU unit. Shirley and I were less than twenty-fours removed from our flight out of San Juan, Puerto Rico and the end of what I thought was the beginning of my retirement and a different chapter of my life.

In the back of the ICU room, there is a large panel of windows looking down on the busy streets and a small park. There were trees in fall foliage, the last of the year's dressings reminding us that winter was coming and nature would slumber. Bright yellow and orange colors costumed each leaf beautifully for their last dance, their last flutter in the wind on the way to where all leaves go when they escape the grasp of a limb or stem. For a minute, just a minute I was able to gain a bit of balance, see beyond the moment until the incessant hiss and bur ump of the ventilator brought me back to the sterile atmosphere I was trapped in with my family. Kendra had been intubated with the ventilator. Various lines ran from a bank of PCA (patient-controlled analgesia) pumps. Each pump sent medication through transparent tubes into an IV in Kendra's body.

Above her mounted on a metal tract, a monitor illuminated a diagram that displayed continuous updates concerning different vitals measured instantly. Blood pressure components visible by lines undulated every time her heart beat. Systolic pressure, when the heart tightens or contracts to get ready to pump blood through the heart into the body, is when the heart is at its highest point of exertion pushing blood into the body. Diastolic pressure measures the lowest point of pressure in the arteries while it briefly rests. Respiration is measured by summing up the number of times a person breathed. Kendra's rate was high, totally understandable because of the assistance she was given to breathe. It was not a real indication of how she was actually breathing because she was unable to breathe much on her own at that moment.

Body temperature was measured by a monitor on one of her fingers. A line ran from the finger attachment to the unit. It indicated her temperature was over 102 at the time I first saw the reading. The vitals monitor can be rather intimidating for a person seeing it for the first time. It is a way to instantly see the progression of a patient's situation. It told me that Kendra was in critical condition. The medications hanging from an IV pole were familiar and unfamiliar to me. At least three different bags hung from the IV pole and the PCA pumps told me that other medications were being delivered in salvoes to combat the disease that was attacking her body. One IV bag contained Sodium Chloride, a standard fluid used to help Kendra stay hydrated. What I saw jarred me back into my work character when I was a teacher. That "professional" demeanor would clash and joust with my fatherly side for most of the duration of our stay in Birmingham.

Fifteen minutes evaporated and the nurse who was tending to Kendra reminded me it was time to leave the room. I would be able to see her later that evening. I walked over to the wash basin and removed my mask, then my gown, and lastly peeled my gloves off backwards dropping them all in the hazardous waste bin. I washed my hands, noticing the hot water was extremely hot. I made a mental note to turn on the cold water next time before I turned on the hot water. The pressure door slid open. I turned left and walked through a short hallway out to the waiting area where Shirley waited. In a while, Ed came out and we decided to get something to eat.

We ventured out to look for a place to eat in the UAB hospital complex. People walked briskly. Most of them were employees, not always recognizable by their dress. This was a teaching facility, a research facility, an intensive care facility along with an entire children's hospital and buildings upon buildings of specializations. Signs at one intersection pointed to a cafeteria. Off we went walking and walking, then entered an elevator to another floor where we exited and began walking up a slight incline into the cafeteria. We were tired, stressed, exhausted and the food was warm and in some cases warmed over, but it didn't matter. We ate quietly, the way we would eat often because there was only one subject on our minds and we didn't know what to say to each other.

We had to come to Birmingham so quickly that we didn't have any idea what to bring or where to stay. We only wanted to get to Kendra as soon as we could. We slept in the waiting area that night and for close to a week after that. We became adept at putting chairs together so that we could stretch out. We learned from others who had been there longer than us how to acquire a blanket and pillow. We worked on taking turns going to see Kendra while one or two of us went to eat or get food for the others.

During those first days from November 13 to November 15, we waited for Kendra to improve to a point that we could see her awake and she could hear our voices. Each day we took turns in her room. As her vitals began to rally, we were allowed to stay as long as we wanted as long as one of us would leave occasionally so that there were only two of us in the room. Our stay in the isolation room separated us from the other patients. We lived in a world looking out on another world where patients were lined in beds from one end of the room to the other. Family and friends visited and stayed, some longer than others. I could not hear anything said, but faces and body language told me to some degree how each person was mending or not recovering. Behind me out the large window, leaves continued to fall from the trees, turning a pale orange or yellow. Leaves cartwheeled off the grass and onto the avenue gathering in dark groups. Suddenly the leaves lifted in a unified flight down the road and eventually out of sight.

Night was difficult. The lights on the unit sank into an artificial sunset darkening everything outside our glassed wall. The sound of Kendra's respirator beat out a hissing measured rhythm, pressing air into her lungs and recovering to press more air on the next beat. Her PCA pumps all quietly clicked out a measured cadence, one slightly different from the other. When the measured medication was exhausted, the pump sounded like a clock being wound and an alarm sounded to let the nurse know that it was time to secure the line and either lock the line or add more medication. The only thing that broke the maddening order of the pumps and machines was the quiet music we might have playing on the television. We all liked music and even if Kendra was too far away in her own mind and place we hoped she could hear the music. She loved music. God had blessed her with a beautiful voice and the resolve to refine her talent so that others could enjoy it.

When Kendra began the sixth grade, I took her to downtown Pensacola to audition for the newly established Pensacola Children's Chorus. She was accepted. Little did I know how much influence the chorus would have on her life. During some of the large audience shows, she was a soloist. Our favorite song she sang was "Memories" from the musical *Cats*, her first true solo with the chorus. Later on, friends told us how much they enjoyed Kendra singing "Don't Cry for me Argentina" from the musical *Evita*. Her voice was unique in that it was neither soprano nor alto. She could sing in both registers as long as they were not very high or low notes. Her training allowed her to obtain a voice scholarship at the University of Central Florida. A year later, she auditioned for the musical voice program at Florida State University and earned a scholarship. As much as she loved to sing, she switched her major to marketing and returned to Pensacola to the University of West Florida where she graduated with a bachelor of arts. Her skills in communication and writing led to a position at a local accounting firm, Saltmarsh, Cleveland, and Gund, where she was employed when she experienced the beginning of her declining health.

I often thought about the intubation and the possibilities that resulted from the tubing irritating her throat. I thought about everything and nothing. I was too tired from sleeping on chairs and too alert to keep my thoughts arranged this early in our stay. I was afraid because I could see how perilously close Kendra's body was to complete failure.

Here was my daughter, days ago healthy and ready to deliver her first child. Now after an emergency Caesarean delivery, her body was trying to close down. This was complicated by her post surgery and the possibility of other problems arising from that surgery. I prayed. I begged. I made wild promises to myself. In my weariness, I asked for the impossible, for Kendra to wake up and be better, much better.

Outside of the surreal world where Kendra was, we searched for more food, for something to sustain us in the night and for a place to lay our heads down. Our needs were secondary to what we wanted to do for our daughter. It was sometime during the third or fourth day we were camped outside the CICU that a hospital social worker came to see us and offered us information on local places to stay. This was welcome news. It also made us realize we were in a long haul hospitalization stay and that recovery could take more than a week. We were given information pamphlets about the hospital and the services it provided for families staying in Birmingham as well as the names of a few places to stay. We called a couple of places and struck out on the first two we contacted. The third place we were told we could rent a room that is usually rented for two people if we didn't mind a folding bed. Our feeling was that it would work and that a shower would help our morale too. As it turned out, the apartment where we first stayed was a couple of blocks from the hospital entry through the old Hillman building, the original hospital that was swallowed up by the complex now called UAB Medical Center. Our first few days were in a Spartan apartment with few amenities. It didn't matter though. We were there to shower, maybe eat and rest.

We began a loosely structured life walking from the University Townhouse to Kendra's unit. We ate in shifts most of the time and slept in shifts in our little apartment. There was little thought about our own needs in these early days of Kendra's journey. We were beginning to wear down. The adrenalin of the early days of the crisis was wearing off.

At a time when we most needed it, the Birmingham Baptist Association (BBA) reached out to us. The churches in the Birmingham, Alabama area sponsored rooms in the University Townhouse where we were staying. Unknown to us, there was an available room on another floor and we would soon move to a sponsored room.

Among a number of people who helped us, two people entered our lives who helped us persevere through our stay. Carol Miller was a representative for the BBA. She also had a sense of when we needed something. At times, she made us dinner and provided necessities that helped our minds stay focused on Kendra. It so happened that Carol was from Milton, Florida, the town just east of where we live in Pace. Carol knew some members of our church, Immanuel Baptist in Pace. The feeling that we were not completely alone in Birmingham gave us a surge of energy. Carol's presence helped all of us though we only saw her a couple times during our stay. Her spirit was expressed through all she did for us. She happened to come by to drop off some food one day when I was in the apartment. I found that my feelings would surface when I was alone. I could cry or pray out loud or be as quiet as I needed. Carol was a blessing that happened at the right time. We had been through a difficult time with Kendra the night before Carol visited. Her calming presence, her prayer and the way Carol encouraged me helped me through that moment and through that day. The isolation of being somewhere unfamiliar was difficult. The isolation we felt individually layered on our other concerns could sometimes sap all the energy we had. Though we were tired, we wanted to be positive and fresh for Kendra when she woke up.

Reynard McMillian was the director of apartments for the Birmingham

Baptist Apartments floor in the University Townhouse. Reynard has a perpetual positive outlook on everything. He almost glowed with joy and would always have a good word to say to everyone he saw. I spent time in his office talking. On those mornings when I would wake up in the apartment after a night with Kendra, I would see Mr. McMillian. His office was at the end of our hall where our apartment was located. He was never too busy to listen to me. His wisdom and ability to listen was a Godsend for me. His experience not only with the people he met in the Townhouse, but also in the journey of life in Birmingham, Alabama meant he had a unique view on the human experience. He was perhaps one of the strongest people I ever met and I was privileged to be in his presence. He was placed there for a reason, placed to see the suffering of people and offer the light of God's mercy to anyone who needed it. I often wondered how he took care of himself. I knew how difficult it was to listen and offer comfort to those who were hurting and afraid. He simply put his needs in God's hands and all the other complexities of life he gave over to the spirit. I remember this gentleman with gracious and humble memories for his strength and beautiful spirit.

One other person that I talked to off and on was Wendy Walters. Wendy is a Clinical Social Worker and Family Support worker at UAB. She could listen to me objectively and sometimes tell me the hard things I knew but sometimes did not want to accept. I took more of her time than I should have. She helped me keep my composure at times when I knew more about what was going on with Kendra than Shirley and Ed knew. The medical knowledge I gained in my years working as a hospital teacher was both helpful and burdensome. It gave me a different mindset and perspective on our journey in Birmingham. It also meant I could not just say what I felt to Shirley and Ed or for that matter the medical staff. Wendy listened and gave me a different way to think about what was going on with Kendra and my interaction with family and staff. I found that I had to be in my professional mind often with Kendra because I think my family needed to know I was calm. I was dealing with what they were dealing with as much as I could without losing my personal emotions. This was an incredible test of my faith, my love, and my will. I am an emotional person and the last week or so the battle between being Kendra's dad, Shirley's husband and Ed's father-in-law became so difficult to juggle that I could not go in Kendra's room except for a short time or not at all.

There were more people who helped us but we didn't realize that in the moment. For example, some nurses and one or two doctors had the ability to listen beyond the professional demeanor that was so vital to doing their work. I know from my own experience working in a children's pediatric unit that one cannot become emotionally involved with their patients or in my case, my students. The result could make the work extremely difficult. Doctors and nurses need to have compassion and a degree of understanding that did not surrender their own personal feelings which could be fortifying or devastating, depending on the moment. Some doctors and nurses do that with an almost natural transition from compassion to clinical personality. Others would learn in time how to balance that duality of professional and personal abilities. Some could not find balance. Their professional demeanor, while appearing cold and uncaring, was a preferred and crucial part of their ability to successfully treat highly critical patients and bring them back from the abyss of life and death. I learned over the years that how a doctor appeared was not how I measured their effectiveness. It was how they took care of a patient that was the greatest measure of their work.

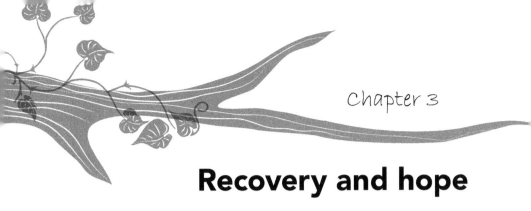

Chapter 3

Recovery and hope

November 16th, 2013

Sometime on November 16, Kendra was moved from the Cardiovascular Intensive Care Unit (CICU) to the Medical Intensive Care Unit (MICU), more or less a lateral move with one ominous note attached. The MICU is where most of the complicated very critical patients reside. Here patients are on a kind of ledge far above an eternal free fall. Some find their way back from the ledge and heal. Some don't. This day, we saw improvement in Kendra's vitals to such an extent that the move to MICU was warranted. Her breathing improved and her lungs were functioning almost on their own. Assisted oxygen was at 40% and Kendra was extremely alert, although she was tired from the infection and affected by the powerful medications administered to her.

The primary reason Kendra was sent to UAB was because of her respiratory complications. At UAB, the doctors were trained to work with a lung bypass. The ECMO system bypasses the lungs and heart to regenerate the blood and exchange blood gases for more oxygen. Kendra's medical prognosis was grave when she arrived at UAB and much more precarious than I ever imagined. When we walked into Kendra's isolation room in the CICU, my first glance at her monitors told me whatever was attacking her body was winning. Her oxygen support was 100%. She was intubated and constantly assisted with her breathing. The sound of her support machines hissing and resetting to breathe for her pounded against my ears.

In the days that followed, we watched the medication and constant vigilance of nurses and doctors. Administered medications and assisted body functions began to hedge the deadly battle in Kendra's favor. Kendra was extubated and her assisted breathing was reduced. She began to respond to Ed and Shirley and me, first with abbreviated eye contact and then sometimes with the lightest touch of a finger and then more pressure from her hands. During the next three days, Kendra gathered enough strength to let us know if we were too noisy. She also let us know if she needed shifting in her bed or needed the nurse to check on her.

Moving from the CICU to the MICU was a major undertaking. The nurses prepared Kendra along with her monitors, pumps, and complex conduit of lines and wires which were all bundled on her bed between her knees and feet. She was mildly awake and we watched her being wheeled down the hall and out of our sight to the MICU. Later that afternoon we entered yet another artificial world into room 8. Here all the walls were glass except the back wall which was the inside façade of the exterior wall of the building. Her drapes were drawn on all sides of the glass walls. The room was much smaller than her isolation room in the CICU. It had an enclosed feeling and everything seemed dedicated to medical care, a sparse and sterile room for patients on the edge of life.

The unit itself had about 30 rooms. Rounds of doctors, both Kendra's attending doctors and the doctors in training, moved from one room to the next standing outside the rooms talking in a language that was as foreign as someone hearing Latin for the first time. They would sometimes open the drapes so that they could see Kendra. With a quiet and subdued tone, the doctors explained the primary diagnosis for the moment and explained the causes and particular characteristics of the diagnosis. At times, the doctors in training asked questions. The doctors had poker faces, some only looking at the doctor speaking, some glancing at Kendra and at their notes, notepads, or phones. No one moved much. No one smiled. And no one gave any indication that my existence or my family's existence was part of the discussion.

The job of the doctors in training was to learn and be ready to give answers. They participated in Kendra's treatment and to a limited degree advised or charted her progress. The doctors leading the rounds were focused on their explanations and questions they would sometimes ask one of the attending doctors. When the conversation ended, they went to the next room to begin a new discussion with the next patient. They renewed their thought processes and examined the charts, focusing on the doctors' words and glancing at the patient or connecting with the doctor's summary of the situation in the room.

We all entered the MICU with Kendra at visiting time. It was just the three of us and because we tried to be helpful and not in the way, I think the hospital staff accommodated us to a degree. Kendra's bed, monitors and pumps took up most of the room. On each side of her bed we had about three feet clearance with a bit more behind her bed. There was a recliner in the back of the room resting next to a vertical window that opened up to a view of the side of another building at UAB.

November 17th, 2013

On the 16th and 17th we saw continuous improvement in Kendra's health. She was awake at times. Her hands sometimes moved and she could motion or even weakly tell us in a husky voice what she wanted.

Her mind was unimpeded except for the obvious effects of some of the powerful medications surging through her body. We watched her respiration improve and with an increase in independent breathing, her volume of oxygen was lowered. Literally, hour by hour, we measured improvement in her vitals. Kendra wanted to see pictures of Meredith so Ed acquired pictures from Pensacola and put them up in the room. Kendra also had a picture of Meredith she kept in her hands. When she rested or fell asleep, she held Meredith's image between her hands.

We attended to Kendra any way we could. If she wanted quiet, the television that was mounted in the upper right-hand corner of the room near the glass entry walls was either turned off or the sound was muted. During this time, Kendra slept. When she woke up, sometimes she looked at us or an attending medical person. Of course sleep was a premium because there were visits by nurses, doctors and specialists. Even the physical therapist made an introductory visit. One of our primary contacts at UAB was Wendy Walters, the Family Support Coordinator we could talk to when needed. As I mentioned before, Wendy is a Licensed Clinical Social Worker as well as an Oncology Social Worker. Her titles gave me an idea of where we were in the MICU. I knew that we had only a couple of outcomes for Kendra. One outcome was good, the other I did not want to think about. Yet I knew Kendra's current state of health could improve or just as quickly degrade.

We saw a rapid improvement in Kendra's physical health and to a degree her mental outlook. Kendra was worn and still battling major issues to breathe and sit up without too much discomfort. She was battling, fighting every bit of the pain and mental challenges she had. After all, Meredith was born by Cesarean delivery just a few days before. Her health had deteriorated so rapidly that she was overwhelmed by her need to be a mother and her need to be focused on her own terrifying journey. She could not talk until she was extubated and even then her voice was a rasping monotone, not the beautiful voice we heard in song.

Today, Kendra sat up in her bed. Her vitals improved rapidly and we saw on the monitors an increase in better respiration and her blood pressure returning to a level within cautious acceptance. Her heart was strong and her pulse was more even and consistent. As Kendra improved, Shirley, Ed and I became more aware of our surroundings. We were less focused and drawn into a small inner place in our hearts and minds that allowed us only to take care of our own needs and to keep a vigil over Kendra. We searched for other venues for food outside the hospital. We began to talk a little about the close call we had seen with Kendra, keeping in mind that we were still miles from seeing Sister become well enough to consider going home.

On the evening of the 17th, I don't remember who stayed in the room with Kendra, it may have been all of us deep into the night or it may have been one of us. Whoever that person was, it was the first time since the 13th that any of us was able to let our guard down and think about our own needs. Hunger, drowsy eyes, and tired minds allowed fatigue to hold us and take us to sleep.

Finally, sleep arrived and I rested. No coffee, no cafeteria food, no long walks multiple times from our apartment to the MICU. Just rest, blissful, blessed sleep. My mind slowed and my fears, though real and still near, was not as threatening. Fears and feelings of total helplessness seemed to lift and there was a clear understanding of my mind and body. I would not have the energy zapping cognitive dissonance that caused my body to work hard to keep calm and level in my demeanor. I no longer felt like I had to find a balance between my mind and my physical needs. I could rest, actually notice what food I was eating, notice how my coffee tasted and actually see that the people that I passed in the hallways existed.

Everything seemed to have a third dimension again, not the surreal feeling of being out of place but belonging somewhere else.

We could see that maybe with time and rest we would all go home together. We wanted Kendra to be able to ride home with us and for the first time, hold her little girl. That was a prime motivator both for us and for Kendra. The journey to becoming a family for Ed and Kendra was a miracle given to them through prayer and IVF or In Vitro Fertilization. Kendra went through the procedure a number of times.

When she told me she was pregnant, we were all sitting at the kitchen table eating dinner. I remember feeling a rush of excitement. I cried. I had no idea the last time I cried, at least not happy tears. Maybe that announcement at our dinner table was the last time tears had touched my face. It had been more years than I know before that wonderful moment I learned we would be grandparents. This was the moment I dared not think about. When Kendra and Ed told me that they were going to have a baby, I felt as though my life was never going to get any better.

November 18th, 2013

We arrived early in Kendra's room when visitors were allowed. The nurses' reports were good. While Kendra's improvement was incremental, it was steady, visibly measurable and in nearly all instances, positive. Kendra looked different too. Though she was pale, she was alert, moving with deliberate meaning. She leaned back on her pillows sitting up in her bed. Her hair was brushed and her hazel/green eyes were bright again. She was smiling though the smile was sometimes faint. Her mind was racing. I knew this because she was quiet in a different way. I saw the face I had seen when she worried and I saw the determined look she had when she wanted to do something and finish the task no matter how long or how difficult the task might be.

November 18th was a Monday. With Mondays, the usual rush of changing personnel, changing menus and the usual pragmatic approach to a new week begins. The doctors in training made their rounds, standing in mostly white attire, mostly stone-faced and serious looking into room 8. Every once in a while a head would nod, or someone would look directly into our room. In the time they spent outside our room listening to one of the attending doctors spin the medical web of symptoms, treatments, and possible outcomes, I felt the only thing I could feel. That feeling was total clinical separation from those who were practicing a complex art of helping life go on or helping those who could not live leave us with as little fear and pain as possible within ethical accepted standards.

The morning plodded along and with our drapes partially open, we watched the world pass by in the hallways. Beds rolled by with patients who appeared caterpillar-like as they were wrapped in white layers of sheets and blankets transitioning from one state of life to another. Nurses, physician assistants, therapists, and doctors, occasionally family members and the ever busy men and women who cleaned rooms and hauled away human and medical refuse kept the hallway in a state of organized discord. As lunch approached, our visits slowed. Nurses set up various medical pumps with long clear tubes wrapped around all the apparatus that was Kendra's bed. At least four or five pumps clicked away. The sound of her respirator hushed and hissed with each assist in her breathing. Drips timed to work at different grams or milligrams per hour ticked away towards a completion of delivery to Kendra's body.

With the middle of the day near, Ed left for lunch. Shirley and I had already gone out one at a time to search for food and just a little time to breathe in and let go of the grip we had on our daughter. Lunch was something we had to do but hunger had little to do with finding food. It was a way to let off a little of the tension we all felt. We could connect with ourselves and look another way.

When we returned from eating, we sat on Kendra's left and watched her rest while the television droned away, a sometimes welcome break from the battle we were all fighting inside ourselves. Not long after Ed left, a doctor and some other medical personnel came into the room to see Kendra. I called for Ed to come back to the room because the doctors had arrived. In a few minutes he returned and we sat down to listen to what the doctor and staff surmised about Kendra's medical treatment and progress.

As we learned by watching Kendra and her monitors, her respiratory situation was improving. Her other vitals were becoming more settled and while they were not all within accepted limits, they were much better than just twenty-four hours before. The doctor looked at Kendra and us and said something like this... "If you continue to improve as you have been doing, you may be well enough to go home in five days or so." I nearly leapt out of my chair. I looked at Kendra and a wide grin came over her face. I thanked the doctors. I thanked God. I thanked the nurses. I tried not to be too excited, a difficult task for me.

Shirley, Ed and I discussed the situation after the doctors gave us the good news. Shirley had been away from work for over two weeks. While Ed's employers were open to his staying as long as Kendra medically needed his presence, Shirley was concerned about being away much longer especially since we knew that Kendra's situation was turning. We all agreed that with time and caution, she would be able to return home to Meredith. We determined that Shirley would go home and that Ed and I would stay in Birmingham until Kendra was well enough to go home. So not long after the doctor's visit, Shirley drove home. We would miss Shirley because there would be one less person to take shifts with Kendra. We would miss her quiet determination and strength to stay awake sometimes when I was exhausted and sometimes when we could persuade Ed to leave the room for food or rest.

Around 5 or 6 o'clock, Ed and I headed out for dinner and relaxed a bit knowing that we would not have to hurry through our meal. We were both excited with the possibility of going home in a week. I know we both reserved thoughts within ourselves just in case we had to stay longer. No one wants to celebrate too soon. We had seen so much happen to Kendra in less than a week. It would take time to sort out all our feelings. Memories of what we heard and what we experienced would take time to reconcile. Nothing would help us more than to go home with Kendra and being life once more as we had hoped. After dinner, Ed and I both went back to Kendra's room and sat down beside her. We didn't talk a lot because Kendra was tired and needed rest. The television was on. The monitors and medical pumps whirled and clicked. I was amazed at how tired I was.

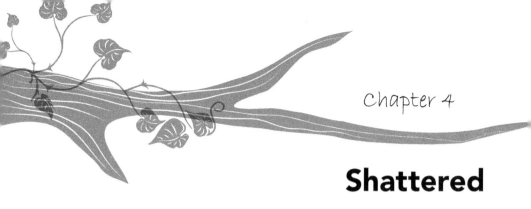

Chapter 4

Shattered

November 18th, 2013

Ed sat close to Kendra in room 8. I sat back to the left of him against the curtains that provided privacy for our room and the room next to us. I was in semi-sleep mode when Kendra's monitor began to alarm a loud, piercing, agitating sound meant to immediately get the attention of everyone within the medical unit. Her vitals, represented by several lines and numbers on her monitor, lit up in red. The frenzied flashing lines activated more alarms. Both Ed and I stood up, caught in the din of noise and sudden change in Kendra's peaceful demeanor. Within seconds, two nurses were in the room and then more nurses and doctors entered and turned Kendra's room into a small command center with each of the participants taking a place in the frenetic beginnings of a battle for life.

A nurse turned toward us and told us we had to leave the room. Ed and I walked out of the room and stood in the hall area next to the supply wall to the right of the room we exited. A crash cart wheeled into the room was already being opened before the drapes were fully still from someone closing the scene from our vision. I looked at Ed and he looked at me. I could see the pain on his face and the confusion that was part of our shock. In less than one minute, we saw Kendra's peaceful sleep turn to something visually I cannot forget. I cannot describe it and if I could, I would not tell anyone what we experienced in those fifteen seconds before we left room 8.

My time as a hospital school teacher in Pensacola exposed me to all kinds of situations with children. After one particular difficult situation with a child, a wise and compassionate nurse pulled me aside and talked with me. She helped me understand that working in the children's unit as

I was doing each day was going to take more than the ability I had. There would be times when a child would have setbacks or great difficulties healing. There would be times when things would happen quickly and I had to know what to do. I had to be able to get help immediately and then get out of the way and let the people who trained to react to life threatening events do their job. I had to stay calm in the moment and no matter how long I waited, I had to stay calm until medical help arrived.

Over time, nurses and techs taught me that I could not keep the things I experienced in my heart. I had to process the event and accept it as the reality it was and move on, go to the next child or next lesson. I was told to put it away until I had time to process the event. While I probably would not forget what I experienced, I had to make that experience part of a memory that would not influence what I did with the next child, parent, nurse, doctor or anyone that I had to work with in my life. Above all, I was told, I had to let go by talking to others if possible and try not to dwell on the memory. Denying, reliving, excessively recalling an event would destroy my ability to work with another child. It was part of life that most people would not experience over and over like those who work in medical occupations.

When Ed and I stood outside the room, we could hear voices talking. We could hear movement and the sounds of machinery and shuffled feet around Kendra. Once in a while, a nurse hurried out of the room and briskly walked or ran until she was in another medical supply room or out of our sight. We were ten feet from the room and we might as well have been outside in the cold air. Outside, we would have felt something real, something we could react to and control by wearing a coat or pulling our hat down over our ears. Outside, we could understand the elements that we had to deal with and react to in a constructive action. In this hall, we were captive to the very nature of a Medical Intensive Care Unit. In these intense moments, our lives were changing but we had no idea how much our lives were going to be altered. Our emotions were pushed to our limits. Fear rained down on me. My mind fought to stay calm and not react to the sounds. The threatening sounds of feet shuffling and alarms pierced my ears as one vital after another dropped. When would this stop? Oh Lord, help my daughter. Help me be strong.

For over a half hour, the activity in room 8 was sustained in a high level of emergency training. I stood with Ed and remembered a couple of situations I saw children endure. Recalling the time I was pulled aside by a wise nurse after one child's difficult situation, I left the hallway and went to the nurse's station to work on my educational notes. I never quite separated myself from that child, but I also did not try to think about the battle waged in that child's room. I was fortunate not to have to go through a large number of emergencies and I had enough sense to stay out of the way and not ask questions. I knew I would learn the child's prognosis soon enough so I went about my business. This time, it was my child and none of those strategies seemed appropriate. I wanted desperately to know what was hurting Kendra. I wanted to fight whatever it was that I could not see but only hear in anguishing tones.

I looked at Ed and my heart sank. My prior training kicked in and I placed my efforts toward standing with Ed and trying to keep both of us in a "wait and see" demeanor. Our minutes seemed like hours and those hours which were only minutes impacted us like hurricane- induced swells on seawalls built strong but a bit too low. At times we were close to being overwhelmed and all we could do was stand next to each other and wait. Time moved slowly while the action before us was expedited by the real trauma that was happening in room 8. Then almost unnoticed, the noise and voices transitioned inside the room to quiet and measured expression. The alarms that screamed at us were no longer calling for action. Nurses came out of the room with tubes, towels, sheets, and things of a more orderly nature used in hospital rooms.

After an hour, maybe closer to two hours, two doctors and some other medical staff approached Ed and me and explained to Ed what happened. Kendra experienced a cardiac episode and the cause was not immediately known. However, the doctors had some ideas and they thought blood clots, among other things, may have precipitated the event. They wanted to do some tests and have a scan done. Ed agreed and so the orders were put into motion. In another fifteen minutes, we were allowed back in the room. Kendra was prone on her bed and the monitors and pumps were once again in order, clicking and ticking, pulsing as they moved various medications hanging from IV poles into her body.

We sat down exhausted, nerves raw and scared. Kendra looked peaceful, but we knew that we had come so close to something we had all tried not to imagine or think. Nurses came and went frequently now to check on Kendra and attend to her monitors. They were doing their job while still acknowledging our presence. We sat and looked at the bed and Kendra's closed eyes and quiet face. Our feelings and emotions were much too tangled to separate. Our minds were taxed to the point of overload. Our bodies were charged with adrenalin and other natural reactions that a body does in an emergency situation. We were tired beyond our own understanding. We sat and waited, prayed, and cried. We just held on.

I had no awareness of the time until I glanced at my watch. It was almost 2 a.m. My head hung. I prayed for strength and wisdom. I needed to understand what I had to do to help Kendra, Ed and Shirley. I needed to know how I could help myself. We sat in silence trying to understand what we saw and what we could do. We could do very little. We could pray and ask God for His will to be favorable to Kendra's needs. We could rest. We could get a beverage or sleep sitting up. We could not will what we wanted. We did not want to be in that room looking at Kendra who was fighting for her life. We wanted to be home. We wanted life to go on like we knew before our lives were thrown into this desperate situation.

Ed and I were asked to leave the room for about fifteen minutes so the nurses could have time to change Kendra and place clean sheets on the bed. They wanted to empty the trash, clean the room, and rearrange her pumps into a more orderly manner. So Ed and I got up and left the room. We came back into the room somewhere between 3 a.m. and 3:30 a.m. Ed and I sat down and looked at Kendra. She looked more restful, almost like she was in a different place because her body was so still and her eyes tightly closed. I wanted to pray with Kendra as I did sometimes. I would stand up or scoot my chair next to her and take her hand and pray.

This time her hands were under the crisp, clean sheet. I had to stand up to put my hand under her sheet to find her hand which was placed lightly on her stomach. I put my right hand out to pick up her hand while holding the sheet up with my left hand. As I attempted to do this, I had to raise her sheet up a little more so I could lean over and grab her hand. I began to reach forward when my eyes were drawn to her legs. At first, I couldn't understand exactly what I was looking at beneath the sheet around her legs. Then I realized with a cold shiver and a deep hollow feeling that sucked the breath out of me just what I was seeing.

I placed the sheet down on the bed. I turned to Ed and said, "Ed, you need to get out of the room." Ed didn't understand what I meant. I put my hand on his shoulder, turned him and told him to go outside the room and wait for me. There were two nurses in the room with us preparing medical supplies that were found on shelves against the wall behind Kendra's bed. I turned to the nurse nearest me and told her to look. I held up the sheet and the nurse looked at what I saw. Then I said, "You have to do something," as if she didn't know what to do. I left the room and within ten seconds alarms were going off again and the frantic organized stampede of doctors and nurses once more descended on room 8.

The cardiac episode was an organized, programmed reaction to Kendra's needs. Once the drapes were drawn, we could hear directions given and the tell-tale sounds of medical machines moving around and people getting into position to help Kendra. The situation was hurried and appeared dangerous for Kendra. This time we could tell that Kendra's condition was even more treacherous than the last time. Nurses ran and made calls. They ran back to the room and the restrained professional voices were still controlled but much more edgy, much more emphatic about what needed to be done. It was six hours since Kendra's last emergency. Now we were watching this happen all over again.

It was impossible to imagine this time we were in much greater danger than the last time we endured this kind of chilling gauntlet. In about one minute, another doctor literally flew into the room with two assistants. We watched as the drapes parted. I glimpsed at the distress that was on some of the faces of the medical personnel working on Kendra. We were in a different place than we were six hours earlier. This was a place to which we could not return if anything went wrong. What I saw in that moment I raised the sheet changed everything about how I was handling our time with Kendra. In most cases, I was able to be clinical in my approach to Kendra's medical diagnosis. But not now.

In the past, I was able to separate what was happening to Kendra from who Kendra was. I knew as risky as Kendra's chances were, they were still strong and could bring her home to her family. I could stay composed and distant from the machines and the sounds and all the other trapping of this artificial world where life is sometimes affirmed and sometimes lost. Now I understood this was my child. This was not my adult child that had been infected by some germs and would fight back and go home. This was my little girl and she couldn't get up. I was her dad and I had better do something. I needed to make it better.

As we waited and watched nurses enter and leave the room with units of blood and other medical materials, we could not find a way to make sense of what we saw. Asking why made no sense. There was no why. There was no reason that we could figure out. Fifteen feet or so from where I stood, my daughter was in a fight that she may not win. Now the only thing that made sense was to survive and be able to get up and see Kendra alive. That was all I prayed for and only later did I understand that was all I could ask for.

Over forty-five minutes passed and the action in room 8 had not slowed. What does one do when minutes become cold darts continually piercing the heart, zapping energy and hope? One does what he has to do or, in my case, what I did. I didn't give in. I didn't hope for anything except an end to the searing pain I imagined Kendra was going through. God, I only wanted peace for Kendra in whatever way He willed. I wanted the pain to go away and wake up knowing I had a bad dream. I wanted what I could not make happen.

All at once, the room began to sound a bit less fevered with urgency. I am not aware of when the activity was quiet in Kendra's room. I know that two doctors came out of the room and addressed Ed and me. They told us Kendra suffered major blood loss and her heart stopped at least once. She was as stable as could be expected and only time would tell us where she was now. We nodded. We acknowledged the effort so valiantly given to save Kendra. We offered our thanks to each person present.

We would have to wait to see Kendra. They needed time to undo the confusion that crossed feed lines and strained monitors to their limits. Staff arrived with buckets and mops to clean the floors. A lady cleaned the bed and put new bedding on her mattress. Three nurses cleaned Kendra and return dignity to her presence. We waited. In a span of five hours, our hopes and dreams crashed down around us. Kendra's life hung near the darkness of permanent separation from all of us. We were beyond shock and pain. We were in a place that cannot be described. Twice Kendra's life had been held just beyond death in a five or six hour space of time. Now, time was no longer measured in hours and minutes. Now, we measured life in breaths and heartbeats.

35

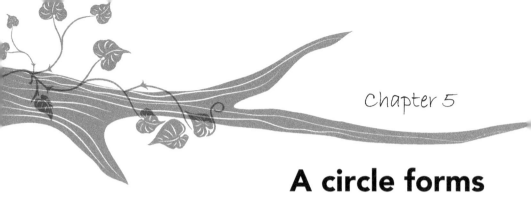

Chapter 5

A circle forms

November 19th, 2013

Shirley drove home the day before when the prospects of Kendra's recovery were optimistic. Now I had to talk to Shirley about coming back to Birmingham. Calling Shirley on the phone to tell her about the turn of events with Kendra was the most difficult phone call I have ever made in my life. Shirley was devastated and was beyond consoling. She was going to drive back up to Birmingham by herself. I asked her not to do that. She was upset. She did not waiver in her decision. I did not want her driving by herself with the news of Kendra's decline fresh on her mind. When we ended our phone conversation, I did not know what to do. I prayed and talked to Ed. He listened. But his heart and mind had so much to digest and bear, I felt I could not ask any more of him.

Our music director at our church Clain Roberts and his wife Cindy were keeping close watch on our situation in Birmingham. They were in touch with us a couple of times and offered help if we needed it. It went against my nature to ask for help because in my past, help always came with strings attached or was held over me later as a way to keep me controlled and doing what someone else wanted of me. I don't remember if Clain and Cindy said they were coming to Birmingham or if I asked them if they would drive Shirley. My memories of those days immediately after Kendra's emergencies are not clear. I do remember asking Clain if he would bring Shirley to us in Birmingham. His answer was typical of Clain. "Of course," he said.

I called Shirley to let her know Clain and Cindy were driving to Birmingham and that she could ride with them. Shirley was adamant about driving on her own. I begged her to reconsider. I told her how much I loved her and I did not want her to face that drive on her own. Our conversation ended without a conclusive answer from Shirley. In the hours that transpired after that call, I felt fear and worry that was taking all the energy and fortitude I had left in me, which wasn't very much by now. I had not slept more than a couple of hours in the last thirty-six or so hours and I was not hungry. All that kept me going was coffee I bought with gift cards we were given by a friend and unknown angels who sent the cards to us.

In the meantime, Shirley started driving to Birmingham on her own. Shortly after she drove off, either Cindy or Clain called her or she decided to return home and drive to Birmingham with the Roberts. Either way, it took a tremendous weight from me and I could concentrate on grounding myself and trying to sort out all we had experienced during the last day and a half. The nurses who cared for Kendra took a bit more time with us now. They knew that our situation was no longer one of waiting for good enough health to let Kendra go home. They knew it was a matter of finding out if Kendra could survive. Going home was no longer part of our thinking during those ragged hours after so much happened. My own experience as an observer for over ten years in the children's hospital gave me a layperson's knowledge of the complexities and dangers involved with cardiovascular events and clotting issues. We were in a terrifying place. Our world fell in on us. Now it was just us, Kendra, and God.

That day, I felt so alone and abandoned. I could not understand how we went from a matter of days before Kendra could go home to a place that was dark, perilous and unknown. The hours had no sense of time or place. I think I may have even been in a mild state of shock because so much happened to Kendra. We spent hours on the brink of an abyss that we could not escape. I could not sleep. I could not keep my eyes open. Fear, for the first time, crept into me. My faith was shaken. My sense of the familiar with all the medical intervention was gone. I walked to the coffee shop and never saw a person or heard a thing. I was living on black liquid food. When I made my way back to Kendra and Ed, a mixture of exhaustion and a desperate bid to stay awake kept me going.

Ed and I were in room 8 when Shirley arrived with Clain and Cindy. We felt a cool rush of air. For a moment, the synchrony of monitors ticking, clicking and measuring medication drips and drops faded away. Clain and Cindy entered Kendra's room and briefly sat with us. They asked us to go eat and I said I was not hungry. It was only then I realized that I had not eaten in over a day. Ed, Shirley and I reluctantly left Kendra's room and went out to eat with Clain and Cindy. I do not remember where we went or what I ate. I do remember we walked a long time. UAB Hospital is a complex composed of older and newer buildings clustered together in a number of city blocks. It has walkways that are easy to find to cross from one building to another. There are also back areas of the hospital with older, less traveled passages between buildings. As I was to learn later, some of those passages were less traveled and echoed another time in the hospital's history with the voices of another place and less technical medicine.

Clain and Cindy walked back up with us to the MICU and entered Kendra's room with us. We spent some time talking and praying. Then Clain said they needed to leave. Only then did I realize they were not going to stay in Birmingham. They drove close to four hours to bring Shirley to us and now they were going to turn around and drive four more hours home. I was embarrassed for what I asked them to do. It never occurred to me what I was asking from our friends. We could not repay that kind of kindness. It was mercy as God's hand was evident.

He has showed you, O man, what is good. And what does the Lord require of you? Micah 6:8 NIV

In my mind now, I know that Clain and Cindy helped us because that is what they wanted to do. In a greater place, they honored God by doing something for God. They extended God's mercy to us through themselves and in that way we received a blessing. We were encouraged by their presence, having been alone in our minds and hearts in a place that was not home. We rested for a few hours. Here and there we took care of our own needs. Having someone come inside the circle that has not been in the battle helped us realize that our own needs were important too. We needed to have structure to our chaos even if only to figure out how we would attend to Kendra. We needed to eat together as much as we could.

Only a few minutes' walk from Kendra's room, our apartment was our sanctuary. We worked out a system where two could rest in the apartment and one would sleep in Kendra's room where a recliner was provided. Each night we rotated so that, in theory, one could get two days of rest in the apartment and one day sleeping in Kendra's room. Our system worked most of the time. Back at our apartment, people watched out for us. Carol Miller checked on us and made home-cooked meals now and then. Carol was from our part of the world near Milton and Pace, Florida. She knew people in our church and she always seemed to bring a meal or some goodies at the right time.

Reynard McMillian, the manager for the Birmingham Baptist Association floor in the University Townhouse, helped us with cleaning materials and showed us where the community room was situated on our floor. On some days, local restaurants donated bread and other food and left them in the community room. Sometimes we went to the community room to get some food when we could not get out to eat or feel like fixing a meal in the apartment. We washed our clothes in the basement area of the townhouse and sometimes waited for dryers or washing machines. We learned to exchange our bills for quarters to run the washing machines and dryers. We began to find a structure of sorts in our lives. We did not know it those first few days, but we would be in Birmingham for over fifty days with Kendra. Everything we learned to do for ourselves improved our own situation as far as necessities were concerned.

During Kendra's days in the Pensacola Children's Chorus, she established some lifelong friendships with other members of the choir. Her best friend was Laura Vanderburg. Kendra and Laura usually roomed together when the choir went on their annual summer tours. They went to Colorado, Washington DC, New York and a number of places in Europe together. They were comfortable with each other, knew how the other person would react to situations and had been there for each other in their journey through adolescence into the world of adults. Now Laura lived in the Birmingham metro area. She married Clay Hammac. In addition to having their own children, Clay and Laura served as foster parents for children in the Birmingham area. They were dedicated to their children and to their jobs. Yet they had more room for the lost, the hurt, and the abandoned children. Caring for the weak and defenseless is a mission for Clay and Laura.

Laura called and asked if we would like a home-cooked meal one evening. She arranged to meet us to serve her home-cooked dinner. Laura must have known how much I needed that first meal because I was especially tired. We went out of the MICU to a waiting area next to a bank of elevators and Laura put down a large basket and a bag. Like the loaves and fishes when Jesus preached to the masses, the food just kept coming out of the basket and bag. Tea, lasagna, salad, goodies that Laura had made herself just kept flowing out in front of us. I know people walking by looked at us in a strange way. It never occurred to us that we were in the middle of a hallway sitting on tired sofas enjoying a meal made with love and care.

Our lives were forever altered. Many of our memories are blistering with the harsh realities we saw and lived through. A meal with a friend reminded me of how God wanted us to know that He cared. He wanted us to know that His will was unshakable but His mercy and wisdom was far-reaching beyond our minds and ability to see how things would unfold. Even now I do not understand why life was shattered and rebuilt the way it has been since our journey to Birmingham.

One other person who was part of our journey in Birmingham was Tim Shuman. At the time we were in Birmingham, Tim was working in the Tuscaloosa area. Tim was another member of our church and was following our situation. One evening he called and asked if he could join us for an evening meal. We were not real close to Tim, but we knew him and we gratefully accepted his invitation. We ate a number of meals with Tim over our time at UAB. He was a welcome change to our daily lives. Always listening, always with a smile, Tim gave us a piece of home to hold onto and reminded us that we were not alone.

Other friends from home wanted to see us. As much as they cared about us, we did not want anyone driving to Birmingham. The truth was we did not want people to see Kendra and what she was dealing with. Her room was stark, as most ICU rooms are for the purpose they are designed to facilitate. Behind Kendra was the reality of her crisis. Rows of pumps each ticking like so many clocks, all set slightly different, soaking the air in different timed registers of one drip or another through tubes into Kendra's body. A monitor screen black with four or five parallel lines of different colors moved in blips and small dinging sounds represented her life in a visual nightmare. We could see her oxygen level, her pulse, her respiration and her temperature ebb and flow depending on what was happening to her body. What we could not see was what was happening in her mind and heart… or if there was anything happening there.

Our lives were inside this small circle of Shirley, Ed and me. Here and there a few people entered the circle, always gracing us with love and care not only for us but especially for Kendra. Outside the circle, many people wanted to enter. While their hearts and love were well- meaning, we had difficulty opening the circle. Part of the reason was because the writing I was doing each day was public and displayed on Facebook for anyone who wanted to see what was written. I opened our journey to anyone interested in reading what we were going through, not realizing what I was creating.

Struggles like we were living are usually not so publically displayed. Most people do not get to see all of the reality that is so blinding when a loved one has gone through the kind of trauma Kendra experienced. The worst part was that Kendra looked like Kendra. One would think she could get up out of the bed and walk out the door. It was what happened inside her and later what became more visibly apparent that we didn't want people to see. Her privacy was everything to us. A few nurses were stalwarts in our struggle. They had the ability to care for Kendra and in a less formal way at times give us a pat on the back, an encouraging smile, and an uplifting prayer. Food sometimes appeared when we returned to Kendra's room. To this day who gave us food and support is unknown. They were angels.

There were other blessings. For example, men from our church raked the leaves in our yard back home in Pace. This was a major undertaking because of all the trees in the yard. It is something I do over the season into the spring. When I drove home, leaves were piled up for me to dispose of when I could get to them. What I could not understand while I was so focused on Kendra and my immediate family in Birmingham was that there was a transformation going on within me. My attitude toward adults has always been very different than the way I interacted with children. Part of that stems from childhood difficulties with adults and my own introverted personality. Now, God was showing me adults could be giving and caring without expectations from me in return for their favors. I could not stay within myself as I would learn and am still learning. What was inside me was better if it was open to others who would help me shape my behavior toward life. Acceptance continues to occur each hour, each day, from one season to another. Seeds were sown and my own weaknesses were exposed through a blinding light that I could not deny.

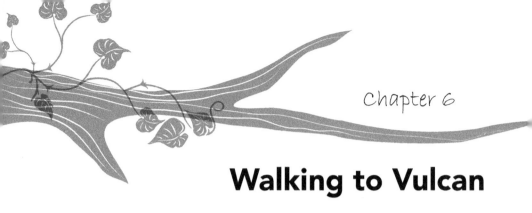

Chapter 6

Walking to Vulcan

November 2014 to January 2014

Birmingham, Alabama is a relatively young city. It grew up engulfing the farm communities in the area. When the iron and steel industries developed along with the railroads, Birmingham blossomed. Iron ore was found in the mountains around Birmingham. The post-Civil War movement filled the steel mills with cheap labor. Steel and iron production began in the 1870s and ended in the 1960s. 1. Nearby on top of Red Mountain stands an iron statue of Vulcan, Roman god of fire made from mountain iron ore.

Vulcan is the largest cast iron statue in the world weighing fifty tons. Vulcan has stood on top of the mountain in a 1500 acre park since sometime in the 1930s. 2. For me, the mountain was waiting. After November 19th, everything I did was measured. Our time in Birmingham had drastically changed. I could not tell Ed and Shirley what I understood about Kendra's medical situation. I waited for the medical staff to talk to Ed and Shirley, but like so many things in life, one hand didn't know what the other hand was doing. I determined that it would be best to wait for a medical meeting so that the knowledge I had could be presented in a manner that was better understood by all of us.

I needed an outlet to keep my body alert and to free my mind. I could not live on coffee any more. I could not eat now and then or not at all. I needed some kind of structure and so I looked up the mountain that anchored Birmingham to the valley and decided it was time to walk. From our townhouse apartment, one could walk most of the way to the Vulcan Park along sidewalks. The distance is a mile and a half one way up the mountain. Red Mountain stands 1025 ft. above Birmingham. The walk from the University Townhouse to the top of the mountain ascends nearly 900 feet.

Starting at the intersection of University Blvd. and 20th St. South, I began my trek up the mountain until I arrived at Five Forks, an intersection of five streets where a number of restaurants, shops and a Methodist church nestle around the intersection. Here is where the Storyteller Fountain resides. According to Bhamwiki.com, the fountain was dedicated to an art dealer in Birmingham who was murdered. The storyteller is a ram that stands in the center of the fountain, holding a book. The ram reads to the statues of various animals that surround the fountain. For me, it was a good place to stop for a moment and catch my breath before taking on the rest of the walk to Vulcan Park.

Sometimes when I walked through Five Forks, many homeless people were present. I never felt threatened or uncomfortable in this setting. If anything, maybe some of the natives wondered who the man was that would walk through two or three times a week and disappear around the curve heading up the mountain. In truth, I often was in prayer or tuning into the natural world that enveloped me. The walks were often in cold weather. Sometimes the temperature was in the thirties or forties. The wind was brisk and it would veer off the mountain because the mountain actually was a ridge that ran southwest to northeast. The wind was out of the north or northwest and literally scraped the mountain, then swept down its western side ruffling my clothes and chilling my hands.

I turned my mind inward while walking up the steep 20th St. S. The street turned and followed the side of the mountain where it changed names to Richard Arrington Jr. Blvd. S. The ascent here was steep and the sidewalk was narrower. The walk leveled out for a bit and I could catch my breath before I approached the old entry to Vulcan Park. A staircase stands facing the road where I walked up to chained gates that led to Vulcan Park. Just below the stairs was a parking area where one could leave their vehicle and walk parallel along the mountain for miles on the Vulcan Park trail. My walk followed the curve leaving the parking area behind me through a pass cut years ago through the mountain. This was not a difficult walk except there was no sidewalk, only broad green and pebble strewn roadsides. If it rained, the roadside was muddy and could be slippery.

Walking on this stretch toward the entry to the park at Valley Avenue, I had to be careful. Cars would come up the rise from Birmingham and accelerate along the avenue close to where I would walk.

This walk was not terribly difficult, but it was challenging. At times, it was quite steep traversing the 900 foot change in altitude from down below on University Avenue. The first time I walked up to Vulcan, the day was cold, clear and bright. I could look down across Birmingham in a broad stretch from south to north. The UAB Hospital multi-complex hunkered down in a large multiple block area. I could pick out buildings and the covered walkways between the buildings. In the chilled air and the whipping wind, I could look at the MICU building where Kendra's life hovered between here and heaven.

I stood still, quite warm from my walk and so I peeled off a windbreaker and unzipped my hoodie. The wind brooded here, hushing and shushing through the trees, almost leafless now. The sun above me was harshly bright, as the atmosphere had been scrubbed and swept of most of the pollution and dirt that is normally present over a city. My ears pulsed beneath my wool cap. Warm under my cap and cold from my eyes down to my cheek, I felt alive, at one with my surroundings. Before me stood Birmingham and beneath my feet the honeycombed mine shafts of the old Sloss mines were silent, no longer humming with the sounds of men and machines, picks and shovels. Nearby on the trail is an old cemetery where miners were buried. All of this took me away from the world I lived in below the mountain. For a moment I was neither in Birmingham or standing on the overlook beneath Vulcan's mighty hand pointing toward Birmingham with a tapered spear clutched in his hand. I was in the atmosphere or maybe deep in the trees where the quiet did not whisper the urgency of each intubated breath my daughter was drawing. I did not smell coffee or stale food. The ache in my bones from sitting and praying and inwardly crying was not present. Here, for this moment, I was alone and I could talk to God in a way that God understood. He listened to my frustration and loss for words. The Holy Spirit interpreted my emotions and murmured those feelings into the wind where they flew upward until I could no longer feel the pain or fear, if only for a moment. Here and only here could I let go of the façade I kept. I knew that I could not keep my true emotions and feelings bottled up forever. I asked God for help. Deeply and desperately I asked for God to provide a sense of direction to all that was happening. I needed help to see a view beyond the hour I lived in and the darkness Kendra was suspended in now. I asked for me and I asked for Kendra because I did not know if she could ask for herself.

As my body cooled in the biting wind on top of Red Mountain, I came back to the stone-floored overlook and turned to look at Vulcan, his head nearly two hundred feet above the base of his platform. I could feel myself falling, the height dizzying and the cold wind no longer woke me. Cold slivers of chilling air whipped my face and chaffed my lips. It was cold. The warmth of standing with the Holy Spirit and knowing God was with me felt far away. So, I zipped my hoodie, put on my windbreaker and pulled the woolen cap down over my ears and began the walk back down the mountain.

For the remainder of my time in Birmingham when I could not hold onto the side of Kendra's bed anymore and when I looked at her quiet face and could not resist shouting for relief, I walked out on the sidewalks along 20th St. South. I began my prayer and talk with God up and down the mountain. Nine times my prayers rose from the shale and red-stoned flanks of Red Mountain winging to the heavens through my desperate, impatient and broken heart. "If it is your will, why is it so awfully hard, so terribly trying before us? Help her Lord. Provide a miracle through your love and mercy." I prayed for hours on end. I prayed when I woke. I prayed as I fell asleep. I exhausted myself with thoughts of how to say what I hoped would be God's will for Kendra. I stood by her as long as I could until the last week in Birmingham.

That last week was too much, too heavy. The pain was unrelenting. I entered Kendra's room two more times. I wanted to see her live and yet, I knew just how remote that possibility was. What I knew and understood was completely stealing my heart and mind where I could no longer look at Kendra. The guilt was real even if unfounded. Before me, all that she was and had been to me and to others was suspended in a place I could not understand. My weakness was not pain or seeing things that would make others cringe. My weakness was the need to turn back time and have everything as it was before. My heart possessed tender places. My emotions, always a liability growing up, were beginning to erode my ability to be unattached to the situation. I was not able to be strong for my family or myself. I was scared now.

I could not see Vulcan at night because of where it stood. Our apartment faced west instead of south and east toward the statue. I knew it was there by its light blinking at night warning low flying aircraft and beckoning souls on the interstate to be safe and careful. Vulcan called me to come and let my prayers fly a little closer to heaven, a little further from where my life was changing and all those who loved Kendra. Vulcan's trek up the mountain increased my heartrate, sucked the breath from me at certain points on the way up, and dared me to complete the walk.

Vulcan commanded me to complete the walk. Put one foot in front of the other and focus on the next few steps. Follow the sidewalk. Keeping my focus on God and my body on the sidewalk, Vulcan's spear guided and implored me. Ignore the pain in my legs. Keep my hat pulled over my ears and walk. Talk to the spirit. Listen for whatever God's will was for our journey with Kendra. In His time is all I could hear. In His time.

But now, Lord, what do I look for? My hope is in you. Psalm 39: 7 NIV

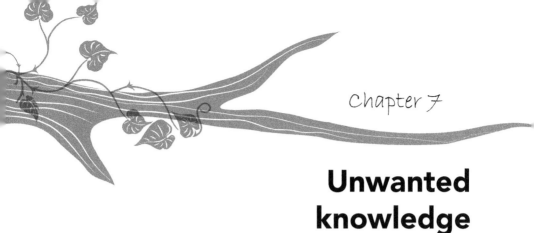

Chapter 7

Unwanted knowledge

Early January, 2014

The medical team worked to stabilize Kendra enough so that she could be moved out of her room to the radiology department. They wanted to take a CT scan (Computed Tomography Scan) of her upper body and head. The scan was going to determine the extent of injury she incurred after the six hours of trauma on November 19th. All of us were aware that this was a goal for Kendra and we anticipated the performance of this procedure.

The timing between stabilization of Kendra's vitals and the actual CT scan could not have been more than a week. The doctors kept her stabilized during a procedure that is performed in a controlled environment under trying circumstances for any patient. The fact that Kendra was heavily suspended by powerful narcotics was probably a plus. A CT scan is administered in a cylindrical shaped machine with the patient lying inside the cylinder. The device that emits the X-ray while it is spinning around the patient is slowly moving on the perimeter of the patient inside the scanner. The patient is slowly passed through the scanner on a sliding pallet. The scan is calibrated so that small slices of a patient's anatomy are recorded while the synchronization of the scanner and patient movement stays in line with each other. The scanner picks up the highlights of a body where a dye or contrast fluid that has been injected into the patient appears darker or brighter than the surrounding tissue. Most anomalies will be recognizable because of the third dimension effect of the scanners' results. With that said, nothing is flawless and results are questionable, no matter what one does.

Late in the night when I was with Kendra, I was rolled up in a turtle-like position on the recliner attempting to get a few hours of rest. A nurse came in and gently wakened me and asked me to come out in the hallway near the nurses' station where I met a doctor of radiology. He told me to step over to the nurses' station where he was holding a folder containing a number of scans. He told me in blunt and chilling words that the results were not good. He wanted me to know that what I would see could be disturbing to me. I asked him a few questions about the scans before he opened the folder and pulled out the first sheet. As I looked at the scan, the doctor explained what I was looking at and what the implications were behind the scan.

He did not have to explain as much as he offered. I could see the results were extremely damaging and there was no human hope of change in what I was looking at on that scan. It was around two in the morning and the news he gave me was a straight forward presentation. I found the doctor a bit impersonal. I did not take it as being rude or unsympathetic. He had information that was heart rendering and the best way to give that kind of message was to be up front and not hold anything back. At two in the morning, I was grateful he was to the point, gave me the results of the CT scan, and then left. My memory of that moment and the rest of the night is much too vivid. The confrontation between my faith and hope and the knowledge of how desolating Kendra's injuries were could not be absorbed in that moment.

The next month, I encountered an onslaught of conflicting feelings contrasted by the reality of the knowledge I accepted. I had a firm belief that God's will would give us the outcome of our time with Kendra, whether that would result in our greatest hopes or our most hidden fears. I already determined I would accept God's will, no matter what. Now I had a human and scientific established truth of Kendra's physical state. At this point, I could only hope for divine intervention. It was this juxtaposition of my faith and my familiarity with the medical diagnosis that sowed an internal struggle inside me about what to do for Kendra and for our family.

Legally, I was not able to make any decisions. Kendra was married and the decision about how to proceed with her needs and care was not in my hands. I grieved for Ed because this is a place no one ever wants to experience. What I knew about Kendra's condition would have such an impact on his young life and ours. I prayed. I cried in the corner on the recliner behind Kendra while the pumps kept pumping, and the drips clicked measured drops of fluid at specific intervals. At this moment, the world I lived in became very small.

Since the beginning of civilization, humans have faced the terrible decision of what to do for another human being when their usual way of life is at a critical place in their journey. There are more questions than answers to this ageless conflict of life versus death. When we can no longer answer what needs to be done for us, someone else must speak for us. If it was as elementary as writing on a sheet of paper what to do and give it to someone for safe keeping, then many people would not suffer through the decision-making process. In our situation, it was not easy. The decision was inconceivable, no matter how much science tells us otherwise. Even the most ardent unbeliever must have pangs and moments of conflicted thoughts. Even if we had a living will, Kendra was young, a new mother, a woman blossoming and coming into her own. She was a wife, a companion of a man who cared deeply for her as she cared for him. The living will could have been helpful. It would not have changed how our hearts felt and the impact Kendra's fight had on our emotions.

Today we have the ability to save lives in ways that could not have been imagined as recently as thirty years ago. We can replace a number of organs in a human body with other human organs or artificial replacements. We can put a patient into a deep slumber and slow their body system to help the body recover from destructive trauma. We can look deep into a body and never even cut a single incision and learn volumes about how that person is healing or not healing. We have the responsibility of knowing whether keeping a person alive can benefit healing or defeat the natural process of decline and death. Who makes that decision? Who says enough is enough? How much government should be invested in the decisions of life and death? When does the decision reach an understandable and agreeable place for everyone involved? In my limited experience, I will offer one opinion. It depends. It depends on every factor that makes you and me and another person who we are. With some situations, the answer is clear. Decisions are made based on the assessment of the patient's ability to recover sufficiently to have a life he or she would deem livable. That is where the law, no matter how well it is written, cannot be balanced so that everyone will be able to accept the outcome. Do not tell me when my loved one is no longer my loved one. The human mind and heart does not always work in a realm of a sterile assessment, no matter how objectively the facts are presented.

I made the decision that I would not make any decision concerning the information I had. I assumed that the medical team would, in a carefully timed and constructed meeting, give us the information I knew. At that time, the doctors would educate everyone about what we needed to do. In the meantime, I would keep my faith, believe in God's will that if there was a miracle, it would happen in His time. If there was not going to be an answer we wanted, it was because there was too much to overcome. For those invested in this struggle for life, there would be too much that could not be understood. Science would prevail and God's will for something beyond my reach and understanding would come out of this tragedy.

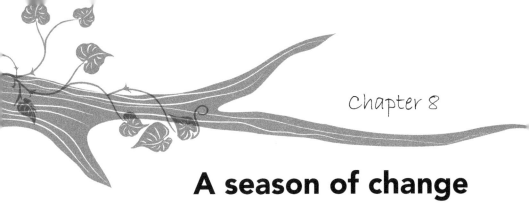

Chapter 8

A season of change

<u>Mid-December 2013</u>

From mid-December 2013, each day seemed to bring another problem for Kendra's care. Her life was suspended in a medical web of treatment and reactions to each malfunction of her physical state. We no longer saw the kind of reactions to stimulus we hoped to see. So often, we felt a hand squeeze or what appeared to be a subtle reaction to our touch or sound.

During the nights I stayed in the room with Kendra while Shirley and Ed went back to the apartment to rest, I sat next to her bed and touched her hand or gently stroked her hair. Sometimes I talked in a quiet voice and told her about the reports concerning Meredith's progress. All of this was having an eroding effect on me. Those days had so many different emotions and mental exercises in discipline and acceptance firing inside me. Maintaining a controlled demeanor, especially after I left Kendra's room, was so challenging that I was often worn out when trying to go to sleep. In those days, sleep was only attained after I was totally exhausted.

Kendra's temperature soared and her blood pressure was erratic and dangerously high. Her heart raced at times. Each of these factors alone would have been enough to deal with but with all of them happening to her already damaged and tired body, her defense system was worn out. For me, the sounds of alarms more and more often brought attention to dangerous changes in Kendra's fight for life. The alarms seemed to reinforce the medical understanding I had concerning her life. I needed to get away from the noise and the constant sounds of pumps and machines. I needed a moment to sleep without waking up in fear during the night or dreaming of such realistic scenes.

Kendra's life was so near transitioning from the mortal to the spiritual we believe exists. I don't believe any parent can reconcile themselves to the fact that their child was healthy one moment and then, in what seemed like seconds, was dying before their eyes.

During this time, Clain and Cindy drove from Florida to Birmingham to see Kendra and our family. I took the opportunity of their visit to travel back to Pensacola. I stayed at Ed's parents where they were taking care of one-month-old Meredith. That meant they managed all the night feedings, all the sleepless moments, all the diaper changes, and more feedings. They gave us comfort knowing that Meredith was in good hands. Meredith was so tiny. A bit over three pounds at birth, she was only ounces larger than when I first saw her in photos. As a comparison, I don't have particularly large hands. If I positioned her body in my hand, I didn't need to use the other hand to hold her. I could hold her on my chest without putting my arms up or my hands on her. She snuggled right into my body and slept.

Meredith's breathing was so shallow that at times I had to check to make sure she was still breathing. After a few hours of her sitting with me, I was aware of how she rested into me, not on me. Her warmth provided a serene sense of God's love for me. I was gaining awareness of how incredibly tired I was not only mentally but especially physically. I would hold Meredith to me and in a while I was asleep. Both of us found in the other security and comfort, and for me, mercy. Mercy lifted me from the terrible reality I was immersed in while I sat with my daughter in the MICU, room number 8. Here in Ed's parent's home, I was allowed to let go just a little. Here I did not grip the symbolic life ring that kept me believing in God's will. For a while, I did not face the battle of trusting God's wisdom and leaning into the facts I knew.

Our niece, Stephanie, was staying at our house to keep an eye on things for us. While Stephanie was at work one day, the toilet in the guest bedrooms area malfunctioned and began to overflow and flood the house. It flooded almost the entire house except the den, our master bedroom, and our work room which were located on the other side of the house. Both guest bedrooms were flooded as well as the kitchen, the dining room and the living room. It is my opinion that darker forces were not happy with our faith in God and how we all were trusting God with Kendra's journey. The flooding occurred when Kendra was dealing with many problems. She was receiving dialysis because her body was partially shutting down. Her edema or swelling was getting worse because her body was not eliminating fluids and toxins.

When I returned home, what faced me were bare concrete floors minus the carpet that had been there when we left for Birmingham. There was a huge amount of work waiting to be done. Much of the work would only be accomplished by physical labor. I stood in the middle of the house and looked around at the bare floors piled with carpet pad debris. Part of the pad could not be lifted from the concrete where it stuck to the glue used to bind the pads to the floor. A strange odor wafted wherever the pad was found. Then there was the disheveled scenery before me. Sofas out of place, chairs piled on each other. There were beds and mattresses propped against walls. Broken bits of refuse lined the window sills. There was a hollowness to the house that I had not seen or felt before. It was as if I was in someone else's home looking at a scene of violence or carnage.

Overwhelming emotions poured out from me and I felt anxiety building so strongly that I had to get out of the house and walk. Outside the atmosphere was cool but not the cold temperatures of Birmingham, at least not yet. Around our neighborhood is about 7/10ths of a mile and I walked it twice, maybe three times before my body leveled off and my mind slowed enough to let me go to a more collected state of mind and body. I needed balance. I needed my mind and my body to be in the same place and not fighting against each other. Then I realized as I walked, I could not do this, not by myself. I could not do this on my own. I needed help and assurance that whatever feelings home brought, whatever was going to happen in Birmingham was part of God's plan for all of us. My part was to recognize and acknowledge that nothing I could do would change any of what had already happened or was going to happen.

While staying at Ed's parents for three or four days, Penny prepared breakfast for me. There was an acceptance on Penny and Hank's part, even though we did not know each other that well. We met and talked a few times but we were not especially close. Kendra and Ed visited both sets of parents and during some holidays we would all be together. As far as being intimate friends, we had not yet developed that kind of relationship. Now, in the midst of all this anguish, Penny and Hank opened their home to me and Shirley when she drove home for a few days of respite.

The Lord is close to the brokenhearted and saves those who are crushed in spirit. Psalm 34: 18 NIV

It occurred to me that if my home had not been flooded, I would have stayed at my house when I returned from Birmingham. Most likely, I would have been just as isolated and distant from people as I was in Birmingham. In my mind, there were forces working to distract us from our focus with Kendra. Not only was our home flooded, our dog escaped twice and once got in a scrap with another dog. Another added distracter was my retirement paperwork had some kind of problem that I had to take care of so that my retirement pay would begin on time.

Being at Hank and Penny's meant I was around people who were already caring for us by taking on the huge task of caring for Meredith. Now they were offering their home to me when I visited. What evil tried to hurt me, God made into a blessing. Later, the task of cleaning up and fixing the house would have its own blessings that no one could foresee. Acceptance of God's will brought far more than letting go of my desires for Kendra. It brought me a clearer picture of what God's grace truly does when one free falls into the arms of the Spirit.

Another difficulty I mentioned was our boxer, Myrtle. She was staying at home because Stephanie was in the house. Myrtle got along fine with Stephanie. Typically, when Stephanie arrived home, she let Myrtle in the house because we kept Myrtle inside during the night. It was the daytime when Myrtle did not have the companionship after work that the boxer missed. Her sense that something was not right was redirected into digging holes, an activity she did not exploit when we were home. On a normal day, I would come home from work and go in the backyard and play with Myrtle or work her through a number of tasks she knew how to do to get treats. Myrtle and I would sit next to each other on the porch while I scuffed her ears or patted her on her shoulders or side. It was pretty much what I did most days when I got home from work. It was good for Myrtle and on some days, it was very good for me.

Myrtle missed our companionship and her sense was that I was not there and maybe she wanted to find me or maybe she just needed to let out all her energy that was pent up waiting for me to come home. Whatever her purpose, she dug out of the yard and got into mischief. One time a neighbor found her and called our veterinarian. Another time, a lady at the vet's office drove to the house and got Myrtle and took her back to the vet's office until she could be returned home. The second time, that same lady retrieved Myrtle and took care of her. What I didn't realize was that Myrtle was given the same kind of shelter I was given when I came home from Birmingham.

Lisa, the owner of the kennel where we kept Myrtle when we went out of town, took care of her until we came home from Birmingham. All of these efforts by family and friends later smothered me in blessings and humility. There was no way to repay all of these good blessings. Thank you is not adequate and so the best I can do is to try to pass on to others the blessings I have been given.

There were other blessings. Men from our church raked up the leaves in our yard. This is a major undertaking because of all the trees in the yard. It is something I do over the season into the spring. These men took it all on and when I came home there were leaves piled up for me to dispose of when I could get to them. What I could not understand while I was so focused on Kendra and my immediate family in Birmingham was that there was a transformation going on within me. My attitude toward adults has always been very different than the way I interact with children. Part of that stems from childhood difficulties with adults and my own introverted personality. Now, God was showing me that adults could be giving and caring without expectations from me in return for their favors. I could not stay within myself as I would learn and am still learning. What was inside me was better if it was opened up to others who would help me shape my own behavior toward life. Acceptance would happen and is happening each hour, each day, from one season to another. Seeds were sown and my own weaknesses were being exposed through a blinding light that I could not deny.

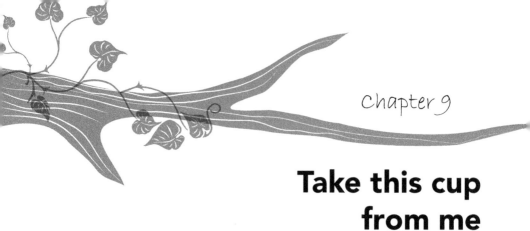

Chapter 9

Take this cup
from me

Late December, 2013

My darkest hours arrived in late December 2013. I talked with a hospital representative about our situation with Kendra. I needed to confirm my own understanding of Kendra's condition and her ability to recover from all she had gone through and was still experiencing. The information I received was what I suspected. Her life was dependent on how much she was supported by medical science. There was very little we could do for her if she were to somehow survive. Kendra would most likely be dependent for the rest of her life on science and the pulse of machines and medications. She would not be able to feed herself. She would not hear us, see us, or know that we touched her. She would never understand the beauty of being a mother or the joy of being married to the love of her life.

I wanted Shirley and Ed to know the facts, but it was not my place to tell them about everything I knew. Even if I could have told them, the information coming from me would be tainted with my inability to be neutral. I would not have delivered the facts without emotion or impartial mind. We all held on to Kendra as long as we could. We all wanted her to wake up and come home. We all were handling our days in Birmingham the best we could. Of the three of us, I was probably the most emotional. To their credit, Shirley and Ed held on to hope, held on to belief that Kendra could come through this. They held me up at times. They filled in for me that last week when I could not go into Kendra's room any more.

The first meeting we planned to talk about Kendra's needs was scheduled and a large number of medical personnel were at the meeting along with Shirley and Ed. During this time, I made my greatest breach of faith and the flaws in my character were exposed. I chose not to attend the meeting because I did not believe we would get the true information that needed to be shared. A large number of people were not only disappointed in me, some were angry with me. They had every right to be angry with me. I had broken their trust. This was the darkest moment up to that time I had felt. Kendra's cardiovascular events, her near bleeding to death, the havoc her pneumonia performed on her body were all terrible moments.

I weathered those moments. Now, when the reality I wanted others to understand was going to be presented, I faltered. While I knew Kendra's life was ending, I could not face it myself when the facts were presented. I fell and let everyone down. The way life unfolds for all of us does not follow the script that we might have in our own minds. There are simply things that happen in life that cannot be explained. We cannot know as believers why good people have bad things happen to them. Nor can we understand why bad people seem to weather life and what we feel they have earned never seems to happen to them in our lifetime.

Perhaps God is the ultimate unbiased judge. He sees the flaws in the good people and the good in flawed people. He allows us to make our own choices no matter who we are, good, bad or in between. When one thinks God should save another, God sees that life must take its course. His interference in the natural order of life has significant effects on people and lives far beyond our knowledge. Do miracles happen? There must be miracles for there are unexplained recoveries, unexplained events that have no apparent reason for their existence. This is where believers and non-believers part ways. I have great respect for science and what it can do. I accept the knowledge that has been acquired and expanded over the thousands of years of medical and scientific progress. I also believe something beyond our mortal presence exists. These things cannot be proven through science or law. Yet I know in my heart and in my mind that there is a spark within each of us that lives beyond the short life we enjoy in this physical life. Kendra was not the first person I was around who faced the end of life. I saw others as they were dying and was present when the transition of some lives from this world crossed over to the life of spirit.

Now, I had to listen to others and take the criticism that I deserved.

Reservations for another meeting was scheduled and we had to prepare for that meeting. For Shirley and Ed, this was just more difficulty that I should have been able to deal with and go through. In retrospect, I believe I had come to a place that I could not accept, the finality of letting Kendra go. I could not face that part of me would be gone and the rest of me would be forever changed. For over a month and a half, life had shrunk to a narrow passage where everything on each side of me, everything behind me and everything before me was insignificant to what was happening in the moment. I lived in an apartment, walked the same path every day two or three times a day from the apartment to MICU room 8. The only escape was occasional forays to a different place to eat and my walks to Vulcan. My heart was put on hold and a more clinical and fact-driven mind kept me emotionally stable and mentally tuned into the numbers that were changing for the worse each day, sometimes each hour for Kendra.

My heart could no longer be held back. The bond between Kendra and me was changing and it was changing for Shirley and Ed. Meredith would never know the Kendra we knew. Ed's life was taking a turn that I could not hold back. The pain he would face upset me. Shirley would lose her daughter, the person she spent time with doing so many things they both enjoyed together. I could not change a thing, could not help anyone, and could not save Kendra. In my mind, I understood what was happening factually. How do we let go? How do we not look back? Could I breathe and not feel all the weight of days and nights of hoping and praying and watching without being able to do any more?

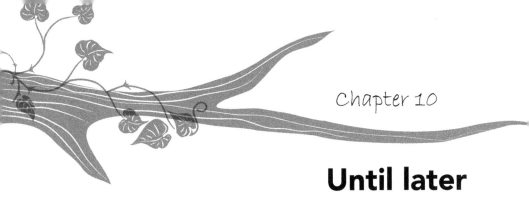

Chapter 10

Until later

Early January, 2014

After the meeting with the doctors, the three of us sat in the conference room numb, devastated at what we heard and had to admit to ourselves. We had a decision to make that no one wants to make. Ed was the one who had to make the decision to let Kendra go. There are those rare times in life when everything one has done, everything that is important to one, their beliefs, their outlook on life, along with the ethical standards each person professes has to be backed up or denied. All one believes or thinks they believe is one thing. When one has to act on those beliefs, especially when those beliefs determine the future of a loved one, the time arrives for character and belief to override all the previous words and proclamations.

We had to give Ed our support and yet what good would that do for him in the making of a decision that he would always have to know he had to make? As Kendra's parents, we had made decisions for her all her life until she was independent. Some of those decisions we made altered her life, changed the way she progressed and grew. Other decisions were less life-shaping and were mundane in nature. Sometimes as parents we had to make decisions that were contrary to what we might have wanted. We knew that the decision, while painful for us and sometimes painful for Kendra, was in the long run better for Kendra.

Now we had no part in the decision that would allow Kendra to transition from this world into the next world. What we tried to do was prepare her for life and give her the tools to make her own decisions about life, about her direction and her belief in God. Kendra's beliefs were well-known in that we had a modicum of assurance at this dark hour that she would be in a better place. Her spirit would live and her mortal body would no longer be required for her journey. It was her presence, her love and laughter, her loudness, her gentleness and so much her care for each of us that we did not want to let go.

After time that seemed endless and fraught with darkness along with thoughts we dare not think, Kendra was given her freedom. We prepared to keep her comfortable and to let her go as naturally as medicine can allow without taking her dignity away or interfering with what would ultimately be her passing into the spirit. Emotionally, I was spent and the signs of PTSD were already emerging though I did not realize what was happening. My body was hypersensitive to the cold and sounds all around me. Hearing Christmas carols in the atriums at the hospital tore into me like a dagger. The thoughts that were in my mind juxtaposed to the sounds of the season tormented me and heaped misery on top of what was becoming an ever-present suffering over Kendra's waning life.

I could no longer go into Kendra's room even for a few minutes. Too many things would happen to me. Emotionally, I wasn't holding up. Mentally and spiritually, I was failing Ed and Shirley and maybe others besides Kendra. There are a lot of explanations scientifically and psychologically for what was happening to me. What it boiled down to in my mind was pretty straightforward. I could no longer sit with Kendra without panic or great anxiety. I was doing no good for anyone including myself. That last week, I stayed in the apartment or I walked the hospital halls which are extensive. I walked in town around places I felt familiar and walked up to Vulcan. I slept more, ate less, cried more and talked less. This was how I handled the impending moment that we all knew was coming. We just didn't know when it would happen.

Our time left with Kendra seemed to turn hours into days and days into months. Then on January 9th, 2013 at about 11: 45 a.m., five days after we let Kendra go, Kendra left us in peace, eyes closed, without any of the drama and crisis that we experienced for nearly two months. I missed her passing by about a minute or two. Shirley called me at the apartment and told me I needed to hurry to the MICU that it was time for Kendra. I hurried to the elevator, took it down to the street and ran to the intersection where no cars were coming. Sprinting across the street, I entered the old hospital entrance going up the stairs past the old heat radiators and across the hall to another hall. I sprinted down that hall and turned once more to find the elevators in another building that would take me up to the MICU. Once out of the elevators, I walked as quickly as I could to room 8 where I saw Ed and Shirley and Kendra.

I sat down with Shirley and Ed. I can't talk about this time. It was much too numinous. This was the last time we would all be together beyond the funeral service. Our lives were no longer bound by human thoughts and actions. No pain I have ever had could explain my feelings.

When we left Kendra later and talked to the nurses about the next step in Kendra's care, they assured us they would take care of her and that all the arrangements for her preparation and return home to Pace would be set up. All we had to do was tell them who would go to Birmingham for Kendra and we could go home. We already knew who would take Kendra home and arrange her ceremony and funeral needs. This was a surreal moment that became days long. Everything we were doing felt unnatural. How does one go from loving and talking to their daughter and wife and then never do it again? What about all the physical effects that were Kendra's? Do they become just things and no longer possessions? I would never be able to feel her touch on my arm or experience a hug around my neck. Her voice and her singing would never bless my ears and my heart. These things do not go away any better than Kendra's mark on my life.

We let go. The next morning Ed got in his car and Shirley and I got in our car and we drove back to Pace. I don't remember much about that drive home. Nor do I want to remember.

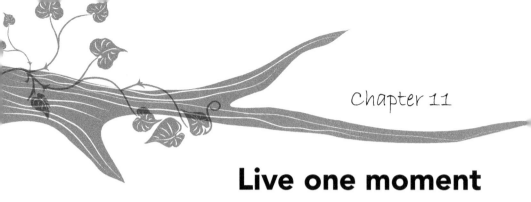

Chapter 11

Live one moment

Late January, 2014

I began writing a journal on Facebook about a week after Kendra was transported to UAB Hospital on November 16, 2013. The journal has progressed from writing every day to about every four to six days. At one time, over 30,000 people received <u>Praying for Kendra Fendt</u> on their Facebook page. At the beginning of 2017, around 10,000 people continue to have the page on Facebook. The number of people who actually click on the page is anywhere from 1 – 6,000. I think it is safe to say the page hit its peak and has since declined. In my mind that is a natural progression of the writing because I think it is only important to people who have gone through the loss of a child or perhaps a relative they were very close to in their life. Others would not have any investment in reading what I write. The time for that writing to end is here. I will continue to write and may start a web page. It won't matter if one or 1,000 or no one reads the page. It will be an outlet that I have wanted from a time that goes further back than our time in Birmingham.

During the past three years, the healing that has taken place has been complicated with the life we live without our daughter. I developed PTSD which is under much better control now than earlier in the journey. The remains of the damage those 58 days inflicted on me are still evident. My mind at times is cluttered. I can be confused quite easily if more than a couple of subject changes occur in a conversation. As much as I try to listen and remember things said, more often than not, I leave out details or confuse one conversation with another.

Every day I still have thoughts about Kendra, often many times a day.

Sometimes I consciously think about her. Other times a situation, a word, a smell, or a person talking or laughing will set off a memory. These incidents can be positive or negative. I don't have a preconceived notion about any of this. I have conditioned myself to be in the moment. My coping skills have become honed so that I can make it through these times.

So, I live in the moment. I do not plan much in detail to do in the future. As I approach three years into this journey, I take one task at a time. I have learned to take care of now and let the rest wait. That may not be the most efficient way to live life. It is the best way for me to live life. The emotions that I have were suppressed much of my childhood because they were seen as a liability and I was directed to control my feelings. In my own mind, it was easier to eliminate the feelings rather than modulate them. Now, emotions are my best outlet for the overwhelming feelings that I have to deal with sometimes. The difficulty is that I don't know how deep my heart can fall. I am learning it is okay for me to have emotions.

I cry, something I denied myself for more years than I can remember. The downside is that I am frustrated easily now. Tears happen over simple things that are almost always connected to Kendra. The confusion that happens in me can lead to anger or to misunderstandings. While this all may sound complicated, it isn't as complicated as it may seem. Only the confusion is complicated. Tears wash away the pain. Tears clear the mind and my heart. Tears tell me that I am past the nightmare of our time in Birmingham. I can see I am still here. I am still able to pick myself up off the ground and go on. Life after Kendra passed away was surreal. It was as if I went from seeing everything in color to seeing everything in black and white. Nothing seemed to fit right. Nothing seemed whole. At times, a moment in my mind seemed hours long. Yet, it was only minutes long. Every day poured down on me and washed me in pain and sadness. Grief is physical as well as mental. Sorrow is not being able to find any happiness, to be lost in the pain and stress that grief brings.

For me, the only way to get through the grief was to go through it. There are no shortcuts. There are only the days and hours of pain that had to be lived until they were no longer cutting me. I had to face the reality of life and all that comes with the unexpected turns that happen in life. For such a long time, all I could see was what I had lost. All I knew was that I was not who I was before. Our family is part of us, connected to us.

Our children are who we nurture and raise to the best of our ability. We make mistakes with our children. Because our intentions are good and children are resilient, they become the person they are meant to be despite our mistakes. We look at our children and feel their accomplishments are part of what we hoped and prayed for them. They live on with a bit of us in their character and blood. And then when we are gone, a bit of us still lives.

It is unnatural for our children to leave life before us. Life does not work that way. The empty place in our lives will heal. The scar will be deep and unlike other wounds, sometimes it will reopen on a birthday, a wedding date, or from a song heard, even a scent. All I can do is live through it, acknowledge the moment and then, as soon as I can, live one moment at a time.

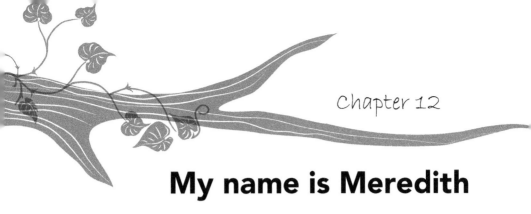

Chapter 12

My name is Meredith

Late January, 2014

Born in Kendra's storm, Meredith showed early on that she was not going to be just any Neonatal Intensive Care Unit baby. Meredith was born into this world nearly two months before she was supposed to make her appearance. Weighing less than 3 ½ pounds, her energy was apparent right from the beginning. Meredith cried loud when she was hungry, so loud that she gathered attention quickly. In her incubator, she thrived and while she was so small that she could be held in one hand, her body wiggled every waking moment. Her arms reached and waved. Her tiny legs kicked and stretched over and over. She was a lively, feisty baby.

On her third day in NICU, she was breathing on her own. Oxygen was rarely administered. Her grandmother "Gok-ee," Penny Fendt, spent most of her time with Meredith in the hospital. Her nurturing and presence provided the security and warmth that allowed Meredith to thrive. While Shirley, Ed and I were in Birmingham with Kendra, Penny and Hank provided stability in Meredith's life. Meredith was welcomed to the Fendt's home where they provided for her day and night twenty-four hours a day. Meredith is here and as healthy as she is because of their giving and sacrifice for this tiny baby. Night feedings, constant care and the wear and tear of watching over Meredith was a challenge for grandparents. Penny and Hank never wavered.

After we returned home from Birmingham and began trying to live life again, Meredith's care was eventually shared with Shirley and me. Every other week I kept Meredith for three days and the Fendt's kept Meredith for two days. Her life has been photographed, video recorded and written about in such detail that other children might not have experienced. While recording her movements, Meredith provided another kind of stability for me I would have never had if she were not here. My life was structured around her life and around my own recovery.

Recovery? Oh yes, recovery. Kendra's loss wounded me in ways that are comparable to having gone through a serious injury. While my physical health may not appear to have been affected, it was affected in ways that are not typical to the normal injuries we think of when one is hurt. I lost nearly 15 pounds from eating less and stressing more. Stress imposes injury that is long-term. Its effect is to damage the future well-being of an individual because it never truly heals completely. Stress physically demands the body to function at a high state of vigilance even after the reason the stress appeared has passed.

Mentally, stress tears down the cognitive processes and allows second-guessing to rise in the mind. It makes the processes of reasoning and thought more difficult because it seeds reactions that are both physical in nature and emotional in expression. Everyone reacts in a different manner because everyone processes and acts differently in situations.

When Ed allowed me to care for Meredith, he unintentionally allowed my healing process to begin. His situation, no doubt, made it easy to look to me to care for Meredith while he was at work. What he and I may not have realized is that Meredith's infant needs gave me a reason to care about myself so that I could care for others.

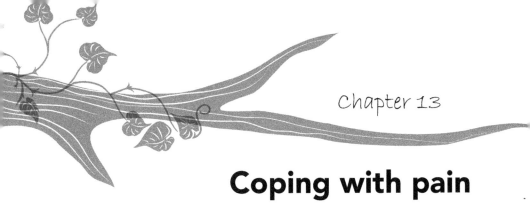

Chapter 13

Coping with pain

January, 2014

When we returned home from Birmingham, Alabama, we had to face the reality of Kendra's passing. The worst part of all this was planning her funeral and celebration of life. We had help. Lewis Garvin, a good friend of our family and Kendra, performed a miracle designing a presentation that personified all that Kendra was in her short life. Our church was full of friends and family.

To be honest, I am not quite sure how I held myself together. Much of that time is a blurred memory. What I do remember is the crushing pain and agony of every minute. There are no words that I can formulate to express what I felt like in those early days of loss. Perhaps that is how it is best described. My feelings were akin to a sickness that invaded my entire being. I could not think clearly because every thought was about the days in Birmingham with Kendra.

The crises we experienced with Kendra were still alive and while I did not know it then, the vivid reoccurring thoughts accompanied by real visions were the beginnings of a battle I still fight with Post Traumatic Stress Disorder (PTSD). My heart races and breathing is difficult when I "see" the worst moments I experienced with Kendra and my family. I have battled depression long before Kendra's loss and it is still a problem that was magnified by the experience. Because I am not an outgoing person, I continue to work on trying to be more open to people and outside activities.

I cried. I cried until I could not cry any more. I moaned. I made sounds that I did not know were in me. Grief and sorrow are as much a physical journey as they are mental and emotional. So what does one do? One holds on. One has to know that as life falls apart, it is also rebuilding into something else that is unfamiliar while it still looks the same from the outside. Life without our child was too harsh, so blaring and loud that even if I wanted to embrace the new life, I did not know how to do it.

I got help. I got psychological help. I talked and cried and cursed and stomped and threw all the pain on the floor for the professional to see. It might have been the one thing I did that I wanted to avoid. It was also the one place I felt safe to rage and grieve in front of another human. My own family was hurting. We were all hurting in our own ways. We could help each other only so much. It was the worst part of my life all over again. In Birmingham, I kept hoping. I escaped for moments. I drank gallons of coffee. I did not eat for two days. Against all I knew, I always wanted to believe that God would heal Kendra, even if I knew factually she could never heal. Science told us that the damage was too devastating to Kendra's body. Our faith told us that in God's realm, nothing is impossible if the will is still there.

The world is changing. Many now do not believe in faith. They scoff and belittle people over their spiritual beliefs. Scientifically, we have no proof of God. Of all the things I did in Birmingham to keep myself sane, my faith and belief that God's direction is sovereign probably kept me from doing some damaging things to myself. No one really knows how they will react when they are in a terrible crisis. For 58 days, we held on to hope. Sometimes it was great hope and in the end, it was love that kept our hope alive.

Now as I write a short three years since Kendra passed away, we are still praying, still hoping for a better journey. I see Meredith who is so much like her mother not only in her actions but in her physical appearance. In our forever altered lives we remain fixed on the journey. There will always be some pain. There will always be some sorrow. There will always be enduring love. I have no idea what tomorrow will bring. There could be unimaginable changes because this journey is not over.

Two years before Kendra fell ill, I had a crisis of my own. Just as I had for over three decades, I woke up one morning, prepared for my day, ate breakfast and got in my car to drive to work. As I approached the highway near where we live, I felt as if someone had struck me with a bat as hard as they could on my left side. Somehow, I pulled over, got out of the car and then the memories are muddled. I made it to the emergency room where I was quickly taken in and evaluated. The pain was ever-increasing, causing me terrible moments of sudden and violent agony.

What I did for the next couple of hours was center myself and try not to think about the pain. After a CAT scan, numerous blood draws and probing, the doctors concluded I experienced an embolism. A clot had formed and lodged itself in my left kidney. While a small part of my kidney is no longer functional, the major part of the kidney is still healthy.

I was spared what could have been, and in my mind, should have been a fatal ending. For a couple of years, I wondered why of all places in my body the clot had gone to my kidney. Had the embolus gone anywhere else, my life would have had a different ending. I was spared. In my mind, I was to continue to live life. My journey was not over. I am here because life still called. I am here to love Shirley. I am here to let go of my daughter. I am here to be a part of Meredith's life and Ed's as long as he needs or wants my love and care. I am here and sometimes I am amazed. The natural world is a large part of our lives. We are healthy and life goes on. There are times the world takes from us those we love.

One of the people I have admired ever since I was a young boy is Corrie Ten Boom. Corrie suffered the fury and terrible pain of living through the Nazi occupation of her home country. She watched her family be torn apart and somehow lived through the Holocaust. It wasn't all she went through that I have learned to admire. It was what she did to live through the unspeakable terror of concentration camps and find peace after she emerged from the death campus. She forgave. She forgave those who hurt her. Her spirit and undefeated faith took her one step at a time to freedom.

Some of Corrie's words apply here. She said, "Some knowledge is too heavy. You cannot bear it. Your Father will carry it until you are able."

We are given our children as a blessing from God. We care for our children, love them, guide and mold them into people who shine in God's love. Some of us will have to let our children go before they have fulfilled their hopes and dreams. We are walking in a season of loss. Our journey is not what we had hoped and prayed for and we cannot understand why.

I will never understand why life unfolded the way it has. What I have learned is not to waste the rest of my life trying to figure out what cannot be figured out. What has happened does not hold me back. It propels me forward. It defines the here and now, not tomorrow or what I think should happen.

Corrie Ten Boom was released from Ravensbruck Concentration Camp due to paperwork error. 3. We may not understand why life happens as it does, but what we can know is that there is a reason for the past as it prepares our future. I cannot spend my life mourning, though at one time I hurt so much that I would lie down and curl inward crying. Grief hurts. Love has to have a place where it grows and nourishes more love. For the last few years, I have directed that love toward my family. I directed my energy toward writing and finding a balance in life. I am afraid of the next step because I have to step outward and live again in the world.

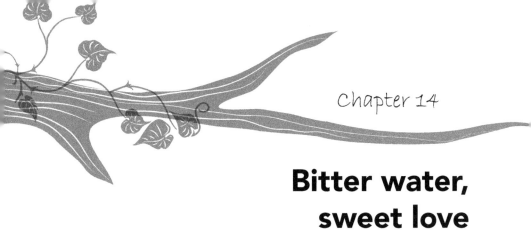

Chapter 14

Bitter water, sweet love

November 12th, 2016

On November 12th, we celebrated Meredith's third birthday. Meredith was so excited that she could not contain herself. She ran and ran inside the community center in Pace, Florida. Her giggles and unbridled laughter bounced off the rafters and walls of the building. She knew this was her day and loved every single moment. Ed's friends attended with their children and they too laughed and trotted about during the festivities. Penny and Hank, Meredith's grandparents, brought a birthday cake Penny made. They recorded the day in photos and videos.

I walked around with my camera and also took pictures. My oldest brother Steve, and his wife Kris also had a camera and video. Without a doubt, this was most likely one of the better chronicled toddler birthdays. Shirley's cupcake tower stood in testament to the love we have for Meredith. Within each layer were homemade icing decorated "M" cookies and butterfly cookies that Shirley's sister Wanda baked and spent time decorating. Ed provided food and drink for everyone.

The tables were set up and decorated by family and friends. Balloons were attached to sticks and placed around the playground a short distance away from the building. The party was a group effort with the decorations either bought or made by Shirley, my wife and Meredith's Nina. Here three years later, Meredith chats and laughs, plays and learns just like a toddler should. She sometimes has fears and when she falls or bumps into things, she cries like toddlers do.

Every day I think about Kendra. On these special days when all should be happy and gleeful, I anticipate the other side of this love and happiness. I cannot help but think about what Kendra would have thought and seen. I see her picking Meredith up when her knee is bruised and loving her, kissing the boo-boo and Meredith hugging her Momma. I see these moments no matter how much I try not to see them. I wish I could not feel these emotions because they are so deep and intense.

Feel these emotions I will do despite my wishes. I have learned not to let them dwell in my mind and heart very long. I have strategies to take my mind and even my body to another place. I have not conquered my emotions as much as I hoped. Because of my past history with displaying emotions, it will always be my greatest challenge. I am not an especially good or bad person. I consider myself generic and ordinary. I am uncommonly common with faults and weaknesses.

I am not as good as many think I am. I am probably not as bad as I often think I am. Esteem takes a ruinous and savage destructive blow when one loses their child. The blame game does not always surface but when it does the finger points directly back at me. Why wasn't I home instead of off on a retirement cruise? If I had been home I would have insisted on more doctor visits. I would not have taken anything the doctors said as a final answer. I would have...

I would not have made a difference really. What happens in life is going to happen. I don't have a crystal ball that can look at what could have been if circumstances were different. I cannot do that because so far in this life no one has ever been able to see the future and change the way life unfolds. We cannot do these things that our mind tricks us into craving. Death invades our life uninvited, unwanted, an intruder that ruins our idea of how we should live life. Then sometimes, against all our good judgment, we want what we can never have.

Losing a child destroys everything in a person's life that is cherished and considered a part of everyday life. Nothing will look the same. Nothing can be retrieved that was put in the "I'll do it later" category. That call I meant to make? There is no one to take the call now. That laugh, the hug, the place inside me that was so full is empty. I can't see her joy, her perplexed look when I said some of the silly things I said. Her anger at the unfairness of this world to the least among us gave me energy, awakened me to my indifference. Losing a child is awful. It hurts and keeps on hurting.

Meredith brings the salve I need to heal my wounds. She allows me sometimes to be brave enough to look at this world and say to myself "I can do this again." I look at her and I see her mother. I remember her mother and I see Shirley, my anchor, my tolerant, loving, forgiving wife. Though the circle is no longer physically complete, it is still bound by spirit and the spark that Shirley and I passed on so long ago in Kendra and was passed on to Meredith. The spirit, the connection is as real as it ever was. We are connected beyond blood. We are part of each other, and with that, a part of Kendra is still here.

Meredith is 3 years old as I write this chapter. We may not truly know what a toddler really knows and understands. My wound for Kendra is open to Meredith. Meredith sometimes asks to see her Mommy. Wiser people than me are not sure exactly what a toddler fully comprehends. I don't know exactly what Meredith feels. I am thankful she does not suffer the developed mental acuity that can accentuate the depth of sorrow and grief I sometimes feel. I do not know what Meredith thinks when she sees pictures of her mother and we tell her that the photos are her mother. Kendra is her birth mother. Kendra loved Meredith deeply and I believe Kendra was very aware that Meredith was her greatest accomplishment and creation. There is no past tense in the relationship between Meredith and Kendra in my world. Death does not sever the relationship between people. What Meredith decides about her relationship with her mother is unknown. I hope Meredith will understand one day that her mother left her unwillingly. Kendra desperately tried to hold onto life so she could come home to her husband and her lovely daughter. Meredith never had a thing to do with what transpired in Kendra's life. Life happened. The reality of life at its most challenging happened with Kendra. Illness does not come to us in a context. Illness happens and sometimes it happens when we least expect it.

One day perhaps, Meredith will read this. I hope whether I am alive or in my spiritual walk, she will know how much I loved her and wanted her to not only be happy but to have great joy. I want her to understand that what hurts so much in this life is healed in the spirit. Like I tried to do for her mother, Kendra, I won't tell her how to live her life. I will try to help her navigate the many pitfalls and traps of life. In the end, like her mother, she will make choices for her life and with that she will reap the benefits and responsibilities of her choices. Isn't that all any of us can do?

Losing a child is wrong in my human mind. In my spirit, I know that I have not lost the connection that is beyond this world of facts and science. I believe in facts and science. I believe in evidence and proven conjectures. I also believe that within me and you there is soul, there is energy that can lead us to who we truly are. We are more than these bodies we treasure when we are young and battle when we are old. We are all part of each other. If you look back seven generations and seven generations more, there is a part of my life that was given to me before I was ever formed. I am part of a generation before me as well as a future generation. Kendra's light still shines in my heart and despite what anyone wants to tell me, she is still a part of me. She is that part of me that is connected to Meredith. My child is part of an unbroken chain indestructible to disbelief, pain, grief, sorrow or rust.

In the simplicity that I often lean on to handle my difficult moments, I realize there were two choices to make for my life. I could accept the way life transpired. I could give into the pain and let it rot my core and take me into the searing pain I endured for fifty-eight days in Birmingham with my daughter and my family. I mostly choose to accept what happened and move on. The complexity of doing this is not lost even on a lock-step thinker like me.

The solace I have in all of this is that Kendra lives in me and I live through her example. She is gone physically but her presence is sometimes intense. She influenced me in ways I cannot articulate. I am a better person for having her in my life. I am better because she is still a part of my life. I accept that I cannot talk to her. Acceptance saved me where sorrow and grief are not enough to ease my heart and purge the second guessing or doubt.

23 For I received from the Lord what I also passed on to you: The Lord Jesus, on the night he was betrayed, took bread, 24 and when he had given thanks, he broke it and said, "This I my body which is for you, do this in remembrance of me." 25 In the same way after supper he took the cup, saying, "This cup is the new covenant in my blood; do this, whenever you drink it, in remembrance of me. 26 For whenever you eat this bread and drink this cup, you proclaim the Lord's death until he comes. 1ˢᵗ Corinthians 11: 23-26

There was and is purpose for the way Jesus lived and died. Maybe there is a reason for how my life has been affected. I do not measure my life against Jesus. I do realize all of us have a calling of some kind and maybe through my journey others can find answers for their journey. Or at least they understand they are not alone. I did not want this. I wanted the cup passed somewhere beyond me. I accepted it because here is where I am and that is the reality I cannot change. I could not find it in myself to pass this bitter cup to another. How could I give my journey in such deep sorrow to anyone and live my life? That is not what Jesus did. It is not what I would do.

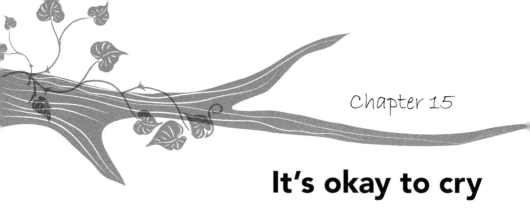

It's okay to cry

January 4, 2017

During my childhood and teen years, I was a military dependent. My dad was an officer in the United States Air Force. From the time I was born until I left home, where I lived geographically depended on where my dad's assignments took him. Moving from air base to air base, we lived a transient lifestyle which was marked by little evidence of our existence in our last home. We left a trail well-traveled by those who replaced us and moved on to their next assignment. It was an invisible road only military dependents saw, a path most Americans never saw or understood.

This nomadic type of life brought certain tasks that had to be performed. Packing home possessions was a well-developed process. Certain belongings were packed into other personal items to compact and increase the efficiency of moving. Only the barest essentials went with us. We lived literally out of a suitcase for two to six weeks after we reached our next assignment. No one questioned the order. No one held out for their belongings. Our lives that identified us were wrapped, taped, and boxed in huge wooden packing crates. Many times we stood on the sidewalk or yard and watched our lives drive away. Would we have everything we put into those boxes when we arrived at the next assignment? Most of the time, the answer was "yes." Sometimes things were missing.

For a child, packing and watching everything that was their identity roll away on a truck was challenging. In our family, it meant travelling with a few cherished possessions. We were told we could not take everything we had. Our toys and personal belongings were expendable. This was not an Air Force directive. This was a family directive. The move that affected me the most was when we moved from Barksdale Air Force Base in Bossier City, Louisiana to High Wycombe Air Station in England. I remember leaving behind my Marvel comic books, my baseball card collection, a bike and a host of smaller less personal things boys my age collected.

Why do I banter about a seemingly unrelated subject and introduce my military background into this journey? In each person's life, letting go of things is part of continuing life. Not only did I leave my personal belongings behind, I also left my friends. Military kids were conditioned to understand part of being who they are is to leave behind part of themselves and their friends. I can say with a bit of confidence that we faced our lives with an understanding that everything we knew would eventually be left behind. That included friends and sometimes family. There was a reality in our young lives that most other Americans only faced a few times in their lives, if at all.

We adapted. We embraced the move because we had no choice. Those who didn't adapt did not do well. Some could not make the transition. We molded into a family within a family. As we grew older, moving on was a polished part of our lives. Moving on was more difficult because we were growing older and more attuned to our friends and their relationships with each other and with us. We learned to say "see you later" when we really meant "goodbye." We exchanged addresses and sometimes kept in touch. Often those connections faded as we moved again and again. New friendships developed and ended.

I have not abandoned completely this kind of lifestyle. I can give away almost any possession without a second thought. If someone needs something, I can lend it out and if it is not returned, it is another part of the give-and-take of life. If I say I am going to be somewhere, I am usually five to ten minutes early. That was expected in my military days. I still do this most of the time. When I tell someone I can help them, it is not just a polite uttering. I mean it. I expect a person to call me because I said I would help.

To this day, to me a home is not so much an extension of my personality as it is an abode. A settled life is something I am still trying to modify in my thought process. Countless homes and temporary residences taught me not to look at homes as a place of personal expression and security. Residences are where we live until we move to another place.

Tears were shed often. The tears were not for what we wanted to keep but for what we could not keep. We cried. Sometimes we were angry, a bit sullen. Depending on our personalities, we withdrew or reached out and grasped the next adventure. It was healthier and much more healing to let go of the last home and friends. Life was tough enough for kids going to a new school. There was no use longing for what had been our lives. Those lives were gone. Move on, move forward. It was best to smile about the good things we had and smile about our new lives we were going to experience.

When our children die, we are in effect packing up and leaving behind a part of our lives we wanted to keep. The truth is we cannot keep that part of our lives intact. We can only select a few parts of life and take it forward with us. We won't see the same things we saw before because life has changed. Our minds are no longer the same. Our minds have to adjust. Our bodies have to alter themselves because of all the physical forces that we experienced with the loss of our children.

Perhaps most difficult is what is inside us. Our spiritual being, our mental acuity has been assaulted. Everything we believed is under scrutiny. Doubt and disbelief surface. So much of what we trusted and believed has been assaulted by the improbable, the unspoken that has happened. That is when I learned that everything I believed in and took for granted was either true or a complete lie. Losing your child exposes all the nerves in your body,

For three years I have lived in the shadow of the death of my daughter, Kendra. It has taken this long for me to realize that while I thought I adjusted well, I only adjusted to the loss of my child. I still need to adjust to being a part of life beyond my home. And there is a lot of life going on around me. My wife Shirley needs to see me again, not just the part of me she sees healing. My granddaughter needs to be given as much as she has given me toward my healing. Ed, Meredith's dad, needs to know I can be depended on to care for Meredith and that I can be trusted to respect his adjustment to life.

During this transition, I have shed buckets of tears. Mental battles have worn me down and built me up only to wear me down again until

I could once more accept the terrible reality of what I lived. My body has been neglected and then exercised and neglected again. Since we lost Kendra, I have not slept well. I have tried to get to bed earlier with disappointing results. I won't give up. I owe it to God, to myself and my family to be healthier, leaner and stronger. This is an ever-evolving journey. What I know is that this is where I am now. That other life, with all of its promise and difficulties, is no longer.

"You can never be the person you can be if pressure, tension and discipline are taken out of your life." James G. Bilkey

I cannot promise life will always look better than it was. There are moments, sometimes days that are like shadows of a previous life. I can tell you that you can go as far as you are willing to walk. I can tell you that when others move on in life, they forget that you have been wounded grievously. They do not mean to be unfeeling. They are living. That is what we have to do. Learn to live. While our journey is not the same, neither is the world and the people around us the same. Life is always changing even though nothing will change the loss of our children. Our wound is deep but we have to understand that it is also what will strengthen us. Our wound heals deeper too. Our love becomes greater. Our ability to empathize is heightened. Our spirit becomes a beacon to others who have been wounded in other ways. We are called to be alive and to show others that with faith, trust, and love, there is nothing that can keep us down forever.

"Out of 132 contacts that Jesus had with people recorded in the New Testament, 6 were in the temple, 4 were in the synagogue, and 122 were out in the mainstream of life." 4 J.K. Johnson

We have to find a way to get back into life and on our journey when we are ready. Each of us is made in a unique way. We all heal differently and at different rates of time. When it is time to get out and live again, we have to recognize that moment and get back out there. Jesus knew that staying in the temples and synagogues would only let Him have contact with a small group of people, some who were not listening to Him and others who doubted Him. In a way, we have to reenter life with those we know we can trust. We need to be around people with whom we are comfortable, especially when we are not having our best moments. It is up to each of us to realize that there will be setbacks. We have to get back up and get on with our journey. Praying, meditating, and investing in something will enrich your life. Give back to life and help someone else. When we give in our sorrow, the return is joy and hope, even in our grief.

I grieve in hope, hope that this journey that has been my life is still worthy of God's love. I can still love life. If by some chance I touch someone's life and give them hope, it is because of the experience I have lived. God's spirit will lift them. You don't see me in this writing. You see the spirit of God. This is His message. God is good.

6 Do not be anxious about anything, but in everything, by prayer and petition, with thanksgiving, present your request to God. 7 And the peace of God, which transcends all understanding, will guard your hearts and your minds in Christ Jesus. Philippians 4:6-7 NIV

I know it is difficult to believe life will ever seem as good as it was before. Maybe life won't have the same kind of happiness. Life can be better though. If we have faith and if we pray, no matter how little the problem, no matter how large the pain, our petition will be heard. In ways that I cannot predict or explain, there can be peace. Our loss will be covered in the arms of Jesus. You see, in the end, it is okay to cry. From personal experience I have to tell you, you can move on. The journey is ongoing.

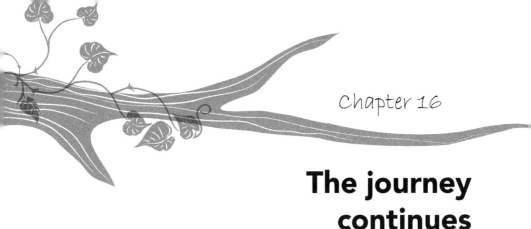

Chapter 16

The journey continues

January 19th, 2018

Two years after Kendra passed away I had avoided writing about my experience. I didn't want to write about the journey. My reasoning was faulty. I was still writing on the page I used to update people about Kendra's progress. That page became a way for me to release my thoughts and feelings. Then I realized I could no longer ignore the weight on my heart and mind. At some point in early 2016 I had to write the book or deny what was to me a calling that God had given me. I accepted His will and wrote what you see now. I am not sure it is exactly what I wanted to say. Hopefully it is what God wanted me to write. Awkward as the writing is in places, it is a view of my journey with my daughter.

There are many memories I have from my entire life that are sharply etched in my mind. None of those memories compare to the time I spent in Birmingham, Alabama with my daughter. When those Birmingham memories surface, they are as real as the moment they happened. In the four years since, I have been able to control most of my reactions when I sense those memories arriving. There are times I cannot foresee the appearance of a memory. Those are often harrowing moments that torment me. I am back in the hospital on Nov. 18th and 19th, 2013 and days that followed. I see or sense again the terrible moments I will never forget.

I survive those moments. Just as I survived the first year after Kendra left us. That first year I was numb, often confused, skittish and uneasy. Grief is a door that opens to let out all the pain that is present after losing a child. I cried a thousand times that first year. I have cried less and less since then. I do cry. When I need. I learned to let myself cry because it was like a cleansing, a release of the pressure I felt inside. Everyone is different and crying may not be the way some let go of their pain. I am hopeful that anyone that has gone through the loss of a child lets go of the pain and sorrow in a positive way. Among other actions, crying is a constructive preparation for eventually getting back up and taking a try at living again.

Now, I feel life is as good as I am willing to live it. Better living means I have to make an effort to see the good in life. A positive outlook has to be established from the moment I wake. There is not an hour that goes by that I don't have some thought or memory of Kendra. Even if I wanted to block out memories or thoughts about Kendra, I wouldn't be able to do that very long in a day.

8 Finally, brothers and sisters, whatever is true, whatever is noble, whatever is right, whatever is pure, whatever is lovely, whatever is admirable-if anything is excellent or praiseworthy-think about such things. Philippians 4:8 NIV

Paul most likely wrote Philippians. Philippians is a guide for Christians to understand what joy there is in being a Christian. As a matter of fact the word "joy" and "rejoice" appears over and over in the book of Philippians. One has to understand just how difficult and dangerous it was to be a Christian. Paul also wrote in Philippians about his own journey which was often fraught with pain and injury. That's not unlike the journey a lost parent takes after their child leaves this earth. Often moments seem to have two sides, the joyful side and the side that brings up memories that hurt. Earlier in this journey, I did not feel that I had any control over what happened to me or how I felt. With time and help from professionals, I gathered coping strategies and methods to stave off the flashbacks that were so much a part of those first two years of recovery.

My Post Traumatic Stress Disorder or PTSD manifested itself in me a number of ways that I didn't recognize at first. I always assumed only people who had been in combat or had gone through horrific situations developed PTSD. My time with Kendra was horrific. I didn't want to acknowledge the truth. The truth of what I lived was part of the denial I had to face. I had and still have trouble sleeping. I dread going to sleep sometimes. This is a battle even now four years later. I have never been a very outgoing person. Losing Kendra only made my introverted character more of an obstacle to recovery. I rarely left the house the first two years. I am better now. I get out, I go places. I give myself a reason to go somewhere. I push myself. Walking this journey is at times intimidating. The methods I learned to deal with these dreadful moments are invaluable. For myself and maybe others, professional help can shorten the intensive time of grief and sorrow. It can make the journey less daunting.

I understand there are people who do not believe in God. They do not believe in a spiritual life. It does not stop me from believing. Those people are not denied by me either. My words, my experience has always been open to anyone that wanted to read what I had written. I have not had negative feedback on the page I write. I don't ask what a person believes or does not believe. I don't hide my faith nor do I boast of my faith. I try and present myself as I would hope God would want me to appear. I hope and pray that those who read what I have written sees beyond my words and finds answers to their journey.

The journey is a lifetime. It began when I was born. It became everything I could hope for when Kendra was born. The journey took me through beautiful days and warm nights. I experienced easy trails and steep inclines, sometimes cold and harsh places. When Kendra was born, my journey became more than a walk. It became a quest to bring her through the trials and pitfalls that one could become ensnared in while living in the present. When Kendra passed away, her physical presence faded from the journey. She is not gone completely.

She did not fall into the past with my memories. She moved ahead of me and she became smaller, more difficult to see. I cannot see her now. I can see where she had been. I can sense at times her passing through the places I come to in my journey. Something else happened. I realized all that time that I was not alone. There are other Moms and Dads, Grands and all sorts of people who have lost a child. They are ahead of me, some are near me and others are visible if I look back from where I came. This journey is populated by those who have lost a child. We know each other sometimes before anyone says anything. We know because there is an open place in our heart that only a lost parent can sense.

It is an exclusive aggregation of individuals. It is not a group that belongs to one race, one creed, one religion or people without religion. It is indeed the most diverse body of people to walk the earth. There is no one in this gathering that wants to be here. I can say with confidence that none of us applied for membership to be affiliated with one another. Yet, each of us would stay with another lost parent as long as they needed us. This company of people come from every stratus of society. The richest to the poorest are here. I can also say that almost to a person, we would have all given our own lives so that our children could live.

Four years after my child passed away, I am only beginning to see who is around me. I am no longer angered by those who shy away from me for a variety of reasons that keep them from talking with me. Fear of hurting me by mentioning my child, or fear of hearing me talk to them about my child no longer is a sore place in my life. I would not intentionally hurt anyone. In fact, hearing someone say something about Kendra is a gift, a blessing to me. It gives me strength to take one more step. Hearing someone say something about my daughter, my Sister as I called her, tells me she is not forgotten.

In the world, most people keep living and after a while they move on from what I experienced. They no longer think of my child unless they see me. It reminds me in a rather cold way that I too have to go on. I too have to live and move forward. Living, reentering life has taken time. There are stops and starts. My hands and knees are scarred with the injuries of falling on my face and getting up again to try and try to keep moving on. I can see the insults to my body. Few others can unless they too have lost a child. Those wounds are only seen by those who have the same wounds. Losing a child cannot be explained to most people. They can only imagine what it is like. I am grateful to our Lord that the vast majority of people do not have a vivid enough imagination to feel what losing a child does to a parent.

Do not despair. All of us, well the great majority of us will find a way to keep going. The burden for each person is different. Some need more time to begin the journey in this next part of life. Others have to find out how to deal with grief and joy walking on each side of them. We are all different. We are all coming to terms with never seeing our child again. Each morning is an opportunity or a battle to move on or overcome the pain and sorrow and find the joy. All of it depends on where we are in our journeys. Time is rarely relevant. What is relevant is the heart and how each heart mends.

And we know that in all things God works for the good of those who love him, who have been called according to his purpose. Romans 8:28 NIV

I would have howled in pain if someone had read that to me in the first year or two after Kendra's death. I needed time to reconcile myself to the finality of losing Kendra. I needed time to let my pain go. I had to learn to let go of the past and all the shadows that come with what we lived before Kendra's passing. I am still learning to let go of my own shortcomings, my invented guilt over Kendra's passing.

There is some good out of all this grief and sorrow. A message from the spirit has been given to me to pass on to others on the same journey I am walking. That message is that we can make it back in life. We have never truly been alone. That if we believe, if we hang on a corner of our Father's robe, we will find peace in some way. There is no finger pointing, no guilt to be owned over our children. Life moves on and on. I do not think I will ever understand why Kendra went from being a young, wonderful and healthy woman to the abyss of life. Then, she was gone. I have quit asking. There is no answer for me. No answer now, here in this life. I accept that, just as I have accepted that Kendra's presence on this earth has ended.

Her spirit is real and in some ways I have experienced a sense of her spirit around me. It doesn't matter if no one believes me. It does matter that I believe and I am not making up illusions. Faith and hope are what I have held onto. I held onto these beliefs when I had all the facts before me that Kendra could not live. I believed that she would go to a place that was so much better than here. A place so much better, Kendra would not want to return, not to me, not to anyone. That is a promise God gave us.

Four years later I am better. I am not the same. I live with sorrow beside joy. I live with sadness beside love. I was angry with God and told Him so. He never turned his back on me. He waited for me to find a place close to Him to comfort me to allow me to understand that in this great journey, there is one truth I can depend on. He will not desert me. You see, my prayers for Kendra had two parts. One was my human pleas for Kendra to live, to recover to come home to all her family. The other part was much more difficult. That part was that I believed in God and that His wisdom, His understanding of everything in our lives was omnipotent. That meant that no matter the outcome I accepted God's will. My humanness lost my daughter. My spirit gained God's mercy. I will always miss Kendra on this earth. I will feel sorrow and sometimes grief will overwhelm me.

I know this too. There is no pain where Kendra walks. She sings better than she ever did. Her wonderful laugh brings smiles to others. Her spirit born through God's miracle is part of me and I am a part of her. One day we will meet again and my journey will be nearing its end. Now, I have to live, be human, find my journey and tell others, life can begin again. I have written enough. God is good. Love, Mike

Acknowledgments

Like the rain in Florida in the summer, many tears were shed writing this book. Every time I turned on my computer to write, tears flowed. The book was already in the making long before I began to write this story. It was born in daily writings during our stay with Kendra at the University of Alabama in Birmingham Medical Center. The book began in weekly writings on Kendra's Facebook page, "Praying for Kendra Fendt." Waiting patiently on me, God's spirit guided me. The spirit brought me to a dear friend, Eileen Perrigo, whom I have known since my early days attending classes at the University of West Florida.

Eileen's patience and understanding allowed me to write the book in the rather ungainly style of writing I often employ. She edited and reedited, redirected me, and helped me through the process. Eileen believed in my story. More than that, she believed in me.

Our time in Birmingham placed others in our path that helped us find a way to hold on and have hope through our daughter's hospitalization. Wendy Walters, a family support coordinator and counselor gave me an outlet for my thoughts and difficulties. She listened and provided me with a different view of our situation with our daughter, Kendra. Raynard McMillian, the manager for the Birmingham Baptist Association's apartments near the hospital, provided us with shelter, food and so much more. He was a positive force in my life during strategic times.

Tim Shuman, a member of our church at home in Florida drove to Birmingham to provide meals and eat with us during the evening while he was working in Tuscaloosa. For me he was a quiet and steady voice, a reassuring presence. Clain, our music director at Immanuel Baptist Church, along with his wife Cindy sacrificed time, money and energy to help us with their love and presence. They provided the face of faith and belief which was personified in their presence.

Laura Vanderburg Hammac, Kendra's best friend from middle and high school, brought us meals she made in her home on a number of occasions. Her husband Clay Hammac was home with their children and a foster child. Her selfless giving was comforting and gave us moments of calm in a time of perpetual crisis.

Jimmy Allen, pastor of Woodbine Methodist Church visited us when he was in Birmingham. He provided prayer, friendship, food and concern for us. Kendra and Ed attended Woodbine Methodist and were beginning to build a church life at the onset of Kendra's illness.

Thank you to all the nurses and doctors who cared for Kendra through all of her struggles. They watched over us and cared about us. Many of them gave us hugs and pats on the back. To the male nurse who provided me with tea. You will never know how much that meant to me. To the nurses who always treated Kendra with dignity and respect, my love and tears still fall from time to time. How good you were to our daughter. Thank you. The mercy you showed our daughter will be magnified in your blessings

Ed and Meredith. You are so loved. Ed, carrying on with all that you have had to do. A new father with an infant. The loss of your Kendra is unfathomable. I pray often for your well-being and that you have a better journey in the way that you need and deserve. Meredith, you are my sweet girl. You cannot know how much you helped me heal. Caring for you from diapers to preschool has provided me with a path to living again. Your spirit, laughter, curiosity and especially your love has blessed me with the strength I needed to take on life.

For Wanda and Bobby, my wife Shirley's sister and her husband, I have no words. Thank you is inadequate to express how we feel about both you and your children. To our nieces and nephews, Cameron, Stephanie, Derrick, Natalie, Stephen and your wife Alison, thank you for being there. Thank you for helping me so often. A special thanks to Stephanie for being so good to us for watching our home and taking care of Myrtle, our trusty old boxer. To the four of you who held me up at Kendra's funeral, I am grateful for your mercy.

To my brother Kurt and his wife Linda. Your sacrifice and love taking care of Dad during the time we finalized Kendra's journey and funeral was beyond the call of family. Thank you for all your support. I love you all.

To my wife Shirley. I love you. Your courage, wisdom, and strength kept me going. You still do. We have come a long way since our time in Birmingham. I pray for you every day, sometimes many times. I wish I could take all your pain away. I am glad you take some of my pain away. We will all be there again. Together. Soon.

To the many individuals whose names I have forgotten, please accept my apology. Forgive me for not remembering your name or acknowledging your blessings. I am flawed and much too human. Thank you for your blessings.

Finally, to the woman who saw me crying outside the elevator. I never learned your name. When you left your children and walked over to hug me, I knew God was watching. When you told me to find strength because my family would need me, I knew God's power to give to others was working. To God, I accept and proclaim to all your will is done.

Notes

Chapter 6
    1. https://en.wikipedia.org/wiki/Birmingham,_Alabama
    2. http://visitvulcan.com/about/

Chapter 13
    3. http://tenboom.org

Chapter 15
    4. Why Christians Sin (Discovery House, 1992). J.K. Johnson ISBN: 9780929239514

CPSIA information can be obtained
at www.ICGtesting.com
Printed in the USA
BVHW03s1651190618
519442BV00001B/24/P